The Making of a Woman

By Jewels

As Told to Marlayna Glynn

BIRTHRIGHT BOOKS

Your Wisdom. Your Legacy. Your Heirloom.

Cover by Donna Cunningham of Beaux Arts Design

Interior formatting and design by Dave Scott

ISBN: 978-1-7372685-0-5

First Printing October 2021

For my husband, who isn't going anywhere.

CONTENTS

CONTENTS

ACKNOWLEDGMENTS

This book has been in the making since the fall semester of 1999, when I met my long-term friend, Kenlyn. My gosh, did we ever think this book would get into print? You've walked beside me during some of my darkest times . . . and my most glorious times. Thank you for always seeing the positives.

Thank you to my parents. Without my childhood experiences with you, I would not have the strength I have today.

Thank you to the hundreds of people who walk the path of recovery with me. I wouldn't be alive right now without you.

I wish to thank my dear friend, Carol, who showed me by example what a successful marriage looked like and reminded me time after time, "Ms. Jewels was very good to you, thank you very much!"

For every man that has walked into my life; and walked back out. You've shown me what I want and don't want in a relationship.

Steven, you changed my entire life. Your faith in me allowed me to shine. Thank you. You will forever be in my heart.

And to my biggest supporter, my husband. When I asked Source for you, I had no idea of the quality of the man who was about to join me on my journey. You are a gift that keeps on giving. Thank you for always pushing just enough so I could taste success. I love you.

Marlayna, Source knew you were perfect. Thank you for your endless effort, patience, and empathy as I told my story to you. Your dedication and heartfelt work are much appreciated.

Jade, thank you for being the unseen magician who made our words make sense.

Thank you to my wonderful cover artist, Donna Cunningham, of Beaux Arts Design.

And finally, thank you to Charn and Jason who will help me deliver a lifelong dream to the world.

PROLOGUE

Hey you! You in the back of the room, who thinks you're alone — I see you. You're not alone. In fact, you're in fabulous company.

Even if you can't recognize it yet, I see that you're an amazing woman; someone the world needs to see more of. Perhaps you're the quiet fighter behind the scenes. Maybe you've only ever heard negative things about yourself:

You won't get anywhere in life.

You won't make it.

You won't finish school.

You're a loser.

A whore.

An addict.

A dropout.

A SLUT.

Yet you suit up and show up every day. You keep fighting and you keep surviving despite what happens around you and to you. I wrote this book to reach the sore spots of your heart. I want you to know you are loved.

Perhaps your heart is broken. Maybe you have been victimized by others. You might worry that you're not enough, because someone said that to you when you were vulnerable. Try not to focus on the surrounding people, you're not supposed to connect with all of them. That's okay. There's nothing wrong with you, and the opinions of others do not shape you. Sometimes you will watch the people who have populated your life grow smaller in the rearview mirror until they disappear. Let them fall away while you keep moving.

I once wore the shoes you're wearing. I hid behind that same kind of mask, because I saw myself as a master chameleon. When I looked in the mirror, I was sure that I portrayed a very well-balanced, confident and attractive woman, who had it all together. But it was a different story on the inside. I strove to be everything that other people needed me to be. I had two identities: the real me, and the constructed me, who others told me I should be. I was drowning in dogma and I didn't even know it. I just kept swimming.

The minute somebody rejected me, I would throw my stuff in a black garbage bag and hit the road. In the last three years before I became sober, I moved every 12 weeks. By the end of my disease, I was very much in my anger and defenses. I was barely surviving.

Now, despite the differences in our stories, I am certain that we all have what it takes to survive. We are all sparks of the divine, replete with divine qualities. Source often interjects by making certain areas dim while illuminating others until ultimately balance is found.

I now work with people in recovery, so I can recognize when others are struggling to flourish. I can sense when they're deliberating their own course and are not quite there yet. My part is to plant seeds and ask questions that get to the root of the matter, to encourage growth.

We all have competing attributes. Ideally, we bring them into balance through healing. Maybe courage is bright and sensitivity is a tad dimmer; creating balance between the two gives us something to work toward. Some people say, *Nope, I'm out. I don't want to be on this path, screw it.* During my first phases of this lifetime, that's certainly where I was, I understand.

When I first discovered my own courage, it felt difficult to recognize it as a strength. Everyone else had always told me who I was. To label myself felt foreign. I was trying to live my life in the "correct" lane according to everyone else's standards. By others' definitions, my actions were often negative. But my mistakes became a part of my story, a product of my path, and the way toward my future. The lessons I have learned have made me who I am today. I understand what's going on in your mind. I'm sure you have the same questions I did.

Why can't I get my feet underneath me?
Why do I keep making the same mistakes?
Why can't I fit into their mold?

Sometimes, I am still challenged by those questions today. So, I have to examine my life, and ask: *Is this my mold, or someone else's opinion of who I should be?* I challenge you to do the same.

The Making of a Woman

CHAPTER ONE

-⁓ ⁓-

The First Quartet

Shortly after my father died, I stood in the muted afternoon sun near a window in his home, scanning the letters and papers and newspaper articles that people of his generation keep. There's an old blessing that says something like: *May you live long enough to understand your parents*, a mantra that knocked around in my head as my eyes took in the details my father never shared with me. Only by going through those musty shoeboxes, full of old paperwork, had I lived long enough to understand the why of who he was. And the why of who I am.

Dad was born in shame, as what was then referred to as a *bastard child* who resulted from an afternoon tryst between his young mother and the man at the barbershop next door to her house. As her belly swelled, I can imagine how my grandmother must have panicked, aware of the perils of being an unwed mother in her day. Sullied by a child born out of wedlock, she wouldn't have been able to get married — and women needed a man to survive financially.

For women of my grandmother's era, the options for dealing with an unplanned pregnancy were few. As was the sad yet all too common choice, she took a vacation, delivered the baby, and promptly homed her infant son with Aunt Mildred in Turtle Lake, Wisconsin. I remember visiting Aunt Millie — *our Mil* —

9

with my mom, but those visits ended when my parents split. When you draw sides, you lose people as they feather away to the wind. So it was with Mil.

Swoosh.

And so it was with this grandmother, whom I never met. Dad showed me a few faded photographs, but she was just a sepia toned face in the background. I understand she passed away recently, just days before her 97th birthday. It's hard to mourn a family member you've never known. Hell, sometimes it's more contrived to mourn the ones you knew all too well.

In Dad's paperwork, I found a letter dated July 1949 from Mil in response to some pretty heart-wrenching questions he must have put to her in a previous letter. On lined stationary that had long ago faded to a parched pale pink, she did her best to comfort Dad in her spidery cursive handwriting:

> *No, dear, I've always loved you.*
> *You always have a place with me.*
> *You are a son to me.*
> *Your mom did not abandon you because she didn't love you,*
> *but because she loved you unselfishly.*
> *Your mom wanted you to grow up without shame.*
> *Times were different then.*

That last line could be the first line of all of our stories. When you slip into someone's history, it's always some version of *times were different then.* It's through this lens that I've done my best to reconcile the choices my parents made — despite the careening direction those decisions took us all. After all, the choices my parents made . . . made me who I am.

Dad told me stories about sleeping in railroad cars and wearing toeless socks and shoes that didn't fit, but I was never sure whether to believe him. As a little person, it wasn't in me to imagine life being so hard. But I later learned that life didn't seem to be easy for anyone in my family. Men could be a hundred percent in their disease of alcoholism and shenanigans while they expected women to marry, to agree, to birth children, and to just get on with the business of life.

Shame was the weapon of choice most used to control, and Mom's father wielded shame with gargantuan force. While he was never physically abusive with her, that verbal abuse might have been even worse. Mom was a healthy, chubby girl, and her father's cruel taunts went a long way in ensuring that she remained thin and ate little throughout her adult life. I dare to say that by doing what society expected of her — remaining slender — marriage was her reward. Paired with her ability to never indulge; nor entertain her own wants, Mom made a life out of famished yearning. I too would stumble along that same path until I discovered my strength.

When Mom graduated from Catholic boarding school in 1964, her only option to escape her father's cruelty and establish a home of her own was to get married. While the Civil Rights Act of that very year opened public facilities, public accommodations, education, jobs, and voting booths to more Americans by making it illegal to discriminate based on race, color, religion, and national origin — women were conspicuously absent from the Act. In fact, women couldn't take out a loan or get credit in their name for another decade after Mom tossed her graduation cap in the air. Mom refused to go back to her father's home, and when she met my dad through mutual friends, they quickly married. *Boom.*

Mom weighed only 97 pounds when she became pregnant with me. She had a small frame and was by then just an itty-bitty slip of a woman. When my diminutive Mom gave birth to me, I didn't arrive on a soft cloud of *babylove*, but fighting for survival. Given only a 20% chance of hearing, I suffered a sensitivity to sound that would later send me running for cover at the sound of a vacuum cleaner or the flush of a toilet.

I spent the first six months of my life in and out of NICU. By all accounts, I should have succumbed to some such thing or another. But perhaps the struggle for my earliest breaths only prepared me for the bigger battles that lay ahead. I would need strength, and I would need to know how to fight.

11

I had long fingers and people would often tell my mom that I would either be a pianist or a pickpocket. I like to think that although I was neither; I was some kind of emotional amalgamation of the two. I learned to play the right notes, and I learned to covertly collect what I needed from others when I could not afford my portion. Emotional manipulation is common with codependence, which is rife among children of abuse. When we cannot help ourselves, we quietly take, especially by over-giving.

Mom's place in the world was slight, and everything about her person reflected her station. She was neat. Quiet. Carefully organized. She wore glasses, which were the bane of her existence; they framed her face, along with her wispy, short hairstyle. They teased her as a child, both at home and at school about her appearance. Back then, glasses were an eyesore: *Men don't make passes at girls who wear glasses.* Mom's glasses were always a point of humiliation, and she resented them, although they helped her see. No matter, I thought she was the most lovely woman in the universe.

My first family was a quartet comprising myself, Mom, Dad, and Yogi, a floppy-eared coonhound. When I was nowhere to be seen, you could find me in the doghouse. There, bundled underneath Yogi's faded red and green plaid blanket, I read to my old hound from my dog-eared copy of *Alexander and the Terrible, Horrible, No Good, Very Bad Day.* I had so much joy as a little person and wanted nothing more than to share it all with Yogi. I felt safe and loved, but I wouldn't recognize the disparity until I was neither safe nor loved. And it was coming soon.

Mom was petite, but big in dreams. Had she been born in another time and place, she would have done all the things she dreamed of doing. Her goal was to be an independent businesswoman and in later years she would try many side-gigs to create her own business. But during our early years together, I'd see her washing dishes or vacuuming, and I imagine that even then she was dreaming of the future she hoped to have. She packed our shelves with books about finance and wealth-building, and I could often find Mom curled up in a chair under the lamp reading about business.

In the meantime, she devoted herself to the crafting popular in the 1970s. She made my Halloween costumes by hand, sewing leaves on my green leotard and painting my face with Frankenstein-green face paint: I was the Little Sprout to the Jolly Green Giant. She made homemade cards born of children's books purchased from the secondhand store. Meticulously cutting each character from the book, she would affix it to the card stock and write cheerful messages such as, "Hooray! It's Jewels' Day!"

When she wasn't crafting, she read books or did crosswords. I loved to traipse behind her in the fields near our home, where she would take a seat on a paint bucket and spend hours sketching an old red barn. I was content to lie back in the grass and read, while Yogi occasionally licked my bare feet. Mom had dreams and talent, but it never manifested into anything. *Times were different then.*

It was Dad who took me to attend activities. I loved to crawl up in his big red pickup truck because I wanted to be by his side, no matter what he was up to or where he was going. I was sure to snuggle up close to him on that long bench in that truck's cab that smelled of leather, cigarettes, and corner-store cologne. My idea of the very best day was driving around town with Dad, as he knocked around the gear shift just in front of my little knees.

Dad was lean and tall; clean-shaven with styled hair. In my memories, he's always wearing a pressed flannel shirt, neat and tidy. I remember that he was always cold. I don't know if it was simply because Mom and I were so quiet and he was the man of the house, but he had a deep voice on him. This, paired with his nervous disposition, made him busy-bodied, and he would fidget when he couldn't control things. He wasn't a violent man, but he'd occasionally bang his hands in frustration on the table, or slam the cupboard doors when he was angry. Dad wasn't the type to break chairs or punch holes in walls. He turned his pain inward; ignoring it until it spilled over the sides. Though our time together was short, he taught me well.

My parents did what they needed to do to make it. Dad worked hard at a failing gravel mill business, while Mom worked a minimum wage receptionist job for a local lawyer with ties to the mob. Despite our precarious financial situation, Dad was in the throes of his disease; he'd waste his and my mother's hard-earned money on booze and other vices. His pridefulness would not permit him to take a handout, and our family began what would become a familiar circling of the drain. We could have weathered Dad's drinking and repressed emotions that bubbled to the surface in an occasional jaw-clenching grimace. But the one thing we could not weather was his attempt at a family suicide.

My little town was in a quiet pocket of our state, especially when the snow billowed down on the long winter nights. We were the only household on our rural dirt road. At night when there was no moon, it was so dark that when I stood at the window, I could just barely see the dim glow of the next house a mile away.

On that night, Mom and I had gone to visit some friends. The adults played cards, while the kids raced around inside, playing hide-and-seek and tag. On the drive home through the snow, Mom hummed along to the AM radio, while I hugged my jacket tight to my chest, watching the snowflakes fall in the light of the headlamps. We returned home to find Dad in the midst of a bubbling-over-the-sides uproar, and I instinctively knew that it was time for me to go to bed.

I pulled on my favorite Holly Hobbie pajamas, the ones with the pom-pom balls on the ankles. Brushing my teeth before the bathroom mirror, I saw my bright blue eyes. Just as everything about my mother was small and quiet, everything about me was white. My hair. My eyelashes. My eyebrows. My skin.

Mom hurriedly tucked me in bed and scooted back to the living room to monitor my dad. She chewed a nail as he placed a gun on the table and took a swig of his Old Milwaukee. He narrated his thoughts aloud as he fidgeted. A raging anger would have been easier to battle, but his disappointment smacked of a rolling lava kind of resignation that frightened my mom.

I adore you.

I'm suffocating in pride and ego in not being able to provide what I want to give you and Jewels.

I can't do this anymore, and I can't imagine leaving you two to fend for yourselves.

I'm at my wit's end and don't know what else to do.

I can't abandon you two: you'll have to come with me.

I did my best to sleep the unsettledness of that night away, but I could hear Dad arguing with Mom about the things that I would later learn only make sense when you're drunk. I stared at the hallway light filtering in under my bedroom door, willing the fight to end. I prayed to ease that feeling that I was about to embark on unfamiliar territory.

I am safe.

Mom is safe.

Dad is safe.

Yogi is safe.

Dad stumbled in to tell me goodbye repeatedly, smelling of beer and desperation. I wasn't aware of the extent of the danger of my situation. Experience taught me that Dad adored me, so I didn't question the multitude of goodbyes. I certainly found it odd. But each time Dad staggered in to tell me he loved me, I answered right back that I loved him too. Yogi was at his heels, whimpering, refusing to leave his side.

Mom recognized the danger of our situation and knew she was the sole buttress against what was looking to be a trio of messy deaths. She remained collected as she navigated how to handle my dad's escalating drunkenness. Each time he placed his hands on the table and pushed himself to standing, her breath caught in her throat. *Would this be the moment?*

He'd turn and make his way to my room to proffer yet another goodbye to me, while Mom would take his gun and throw it over the porch into the darkness. Dad would teeter back again, to his cabinet, to grab another model. His hands would fumble each cold, dense, metal weapon unsteadily — an image that would come to haunt my thoughts between asleep and awake. Within his boiling blood, the alcohol unleashed shame, rage, and the sore abandonment trauma he'd experienced as a child. Mom snapped into fight-or-flight, running solely on adrenaline, as she acted as the bastion of our very lives. While facing him, her eyes darted from his drunken gaze, to the empty bottles of Old Milwaukee, to the gun cabinet, and back again. This scenario played out for some time until the phone rang at a very late hour. It was one of Dad's drinking buddies, David.

"How's it going over there?" David asked when Mom picked up the phone. "Everything okay?"

"Yup," my mom replied, staring straight at Dad. "Everything's ...A-okay."

Her hesitation did the trick, and David discerned everything was most definitely *not okay*. He jumped in his cruiser and hoped to get to our place in time. When he arrived, David saw he needed to sit down with my dad to appease the uncharacteristic malignant rage rolling off of him. Dad slammed his fist on the table, thrusting himself up from his seat once again, then stumbled the short distance to the fridge to offer David a beer, who carefully declined. David was the city sheriff, and he was on duty.

Mom took that short distraction to race to my room, sweep me up in her arms, and whisper in my ear, "We're going for a ride." She wrapped me in one of my blankets, and I reached out to grab my Grover with one hand as she whisked me away. Moments later, she guided our car into that quiet, inky darkness, never to return. For the rest of that night, we were held safe at my aunt and uncle's home. I wrapped up in a quilt that was not my own, beside a warm dome nightlight, making shadow animals on the ceiling until I fell asleep. The larger shadows that would haunt me were already looming in the not-too-distant future, less than six months away: the mandatory waiting period between Mom's divorce and remarriage.

The next morning, the lawyer Mom worked for funded two plane tickets to his beach house in Texas, where we remained until they completed the divorce proceedings. I have one memory from what must have been Mom's birthday. I can see the paper numbers three and zero dangling from a clothes hanger; a makeshift form of decoration, like the fragile future we would hang our hopes from.

Just like that, Dad was gone. His bellows went quiet. His absence created a yawning void that opened its maw for many men and beast to step forth from. Without Dad, his financial contribution to our household, and his company, Mom sailed adrift in a sea, looking for somewhere safe to dock. Some refer to this drift as any port in a storm, but I call that part of my life the ending of Daddy's Little Girl and the slow Awakening of a Warrior.

CHAPTER TWO

Seen and Not Heard

S ome rules create closeness, and some enforce distance. As
a young, twinkly eyed bride, my mom signed a marriage
license that bound her to my father. After decades of living
in a home of exhausted love and twisted blackness, she scrawled
her name across the bottom of a restraining order, and sealed off
our past. Between the Texas coast and our hometown, my father
became a ghost resurrected only by forbidden memories I'd
scrawl in the tiny journal I'd lock away in secret. It was the only
place he could be good. Public shame followed him everywhere.

Mom's lawyer and his pals put the fear of God into Dad, and
in going through his papers, I saw that they made life a living
hell for him. No bank would give him a loan. No employer in the
city would hire or contract him. His gravel mill sunk into obliv-
ion. While Dad became the humiliated, abandoned pariah he
feared he'd always been, I yearned for the comfort of his love.
When I asked about him, Mom gave me one of two answers:

He's busy.

He's working.

Eventually I stopped asking. My first family fell silent, save
the somber strings of loneliness that pulled at us in different
ways. I was five years old in 1977 with one fuzzy friend who I

could clutch when I ached for the wholeness of home. I'd clutch my stuffed Grover as hard as I could, and weep softly into his head, until I matted his fur with snot and tears. Aside from Grover, sometimes I had Mom, when she'd return from dissociating from her pain to be present with me. In those moments, we were a powerful pair, two heroines against the stark loneliness of our lives. Then she'd drift away again, and I'd wonder why she didn't have many friends outside of the people she played cards with. Even at a young age, I could recognize Mom had a tendency to draw in poor company. She'd spend her free time playing cards with her landlords, a crowd that eventually included the infamous Robert.

Robert's poison pooled right below his ominous eyes. Children see everything adults seem to hide from themselves. Mom's gnawing loneliness quickly eroded the line between fear and instinct — until her partially sober discernment became a disillusioned haze. Mom claimed she found Robert *gross*. She didn't like his *macho attitude*. Naturally, she did what women in her position always do — *she started dating him*. Over hearts, clubs, diamonds, and spades, Mom gradually allowed Robert into her life, and therefore, mine. If she'd paid attention to her initial impression, my life would not have unraveled in the way it did; until every frayed fiber came undone through events I neither designed nor desired.

Robert's son, Bobby, was 17 years old the first night they left him to babysit me and his youngest brother, David. Just as Mom never told me what they had for dinner that night, I never told her what Bobby did to me after David fell asleep. And so within six months of leaving my father, Mom and I were moving our meagre belongings into Robert's trailer. I gained four new older siblings: Thomas, Bobby, Teresa, and David. We crowded into the small rooms of the trailer together, one extensive family, save Thomas as he had already moved out on his own.

Ripped from my safe existence and my hope for reunification with Dad and Yogi, they tossed me into a swiftly moving current; everything happened so fast. I fought to keep my head above water and paddle like hell as the massive changes threatened to over-whelm me. The turbulence of my new reality swept me far away from Dad's love, those long rides in his old truck, and Yogi. I was drowning. And for a long time, I felt like my toes would never hit solid ground again.

Gone was my handsome father with his flannel shirts and nervous disposition, replaced by a burly not-my-father man with a tight perm that he wore long in the back. Robert wore an ill-fitting jean jacket vest with sheepskin inside, pulled right across his massive chest. On his right breast was a patch that said *Aries* with a little bull on it. I used to stare at that stupid little bull, trying to make sense of the replacement in fathers.

Robert's kids lost their mother to a brain aneurysm. A prosti-tute moved in to do a short stint as a fill-in mother figure, bring-ing with her the thick energy of sex that permeated Robert, his kids, the household, and never went away. There was sexual abuse that rooted back to Robert's parents, my grandparents, so the prostitute just normalized it for him. And when Mom be-came Robert's wife, I lost her, too. The loving parent I once knew — that stronghold of safety — drifted downstream to a place al-ways just out of my reach. The defenses breached, I suffocated in the disorder of the other children. In this unknown world with-out Dad — nobody adored me anymore. At least not in the right way.

In my other life, our home was open, light, and free flowing because we were a family unit. Even the layout of Robert's trailer defined my new existence. Mom and Robert shared a bedroom in the front, while us four kids shared two dark bedrooms in the back — hidden away in the cold quiet, out of sight, out of mind, and out of reach. Once our parents' bedroom door closed at night, it physically separated us no matter what went on in the back of the trailer. They did not permit us to go into their room without asking; I only had to open that door one time to learn to never, ever do that again.

Before my mom combined families with Robert and his rag-tag children, I had a place at the front of the room; a voice at the center of my parents' household. As the only child, my dad adored me and I adored him. In the confusion of my new life, I shrunk, and learned to stay in the background; it estranged me from the only person I had left to love me, and even when Mom was physically present, she was emotionally out of reach. I no longer wanted to be front and center as Robert severely disciplined the other kids. If they were cocky or showy, he would have smacked them down with his fat-fingered hands. I wanted to be small, so I hid myself away in the shadows — it was the safest course of action.

But while I retreated, I watched. I was still too young to understand much about sex, but I certainly saw the power that held over others. The prostitute had irrevocably tainted Robert's family with the sickness of sex. It wasn't the kind of sex that was consensual or giving, but a forced heaviness that lingered in every corner of the trailer. There was the sex between Mom and Robert, something I imagined at night as I endured my own horror. Even at a young age, I sensed it was a sad act weighted with an unspoken power dynamic; hardly consensual, even in the confines of marriage.

Despite our increasing distance, Mom and I together operated as cogs in a grind for survival. I'd remind myself she loved me, even if her expression of it in our new life felt ambiguous and exhausted. Her previous life with Dad evaporated as she embraced a very challenging situation, dragging me along by the neck. I imagine it was hard to be alone, and even harder to stay with Robert and his kids. I watched my mother become a load-bearing wall to ensure she sheltered us. She determined that if our future was going to be insufferable regardless, we might as well have financial security with Robert. Thinking of all the books on the shelf of our old life, I imagined a sense of stability took precedence over everything else. Money. But even in my youth, I recognized there were more important ways to be stable.

When I look at pictures of Robert kissing Mom, it's clear that she found his touch just short of nauseating. Yet she puckered up and put on a brave face because she determined we were going to survive. She accepted she was going to raise Robert's kids. Why him? Why them? Lacking exposure to other men, Mom saw our small town comprising people she'd known her entire life. Better to take a risk on a stranger.

And so Mom withdrew into the machinations of this life; becoming absent from every level; abandoning herself and me in every sense. While she may have been physically around as much as she always had been, when I needed it most, Mom stopped hugging me. She stopped kissing me on the lips. Her affection for me turned from spontaneous to perfunctory as she became my parent and my guardian in name only.

Once, when we were sitting in the car, I reached for her hand to hold it. She pulled her arm away saying, "This makes me feel weird," after which I stared straight ahead, and coiled my tiny little fingers into a fist, determining I would hold myself as best I could from then on. It wasn't just me, Mom was not affectionate with Robert's kids either. It was very much a stepmother-meets-stepchildren relationship. Somehow I too fell under that umbrella of no touching, and physical affection between Mom and me faded to not much more than a memory.

But it wasn't like the other kids in the household received more care than I did. Mostly, we each fended for our emotional health; out of sight, out of mind — a byproduct of living with two parents who could not meet their own emotional needs. I wondered if Mom ever missed when our quartet was her primary concern. I wondered about a lot of things. I said very little. Each blow to my safety flattened me down further to a squishy ball of unprocessed emotion. Like Dad, I pushed it all down, down, down, and down. And like Dad, I too would erupt one day.

Mom shut down her feminine side. Gone were the fun costumes and the sketching and the handmade birthday cards. It was as if we stepped from one life into another and could bring only one thing from our previous existence along. I brought Grover; she brought her quirky reading glasses. She ruled the roost, and ran the budget, while Robert brought in the money — which was an inadequate contribution.

Mom ate little. When I wrapped my arms around her legs, I could feel her bones through her nylons. She was growing frailer by the day — even her skin and hair looked different. Dried out. Faded. I assumed her withering away was because there was never enough for her. Not enough food. Not enough space. Not enough love. There was only the stench of sex, the bondage that kept us tied together. At a young age, I watched. And vowed I would never fall under the thumb of another.

Rules eclipsed the reality of my mother. Robert was the dictator of the household, with a strict regimen for everything that we were to follow from the moment we awoke until the moment we went to sleep. A detailed schedule dictated everything. Having served in the Navy, Robert had relentless methods of asserting himself over others to control the ranks. Our assignment:

6:30 a.m. – wake up for school, get dressed, brush teeth, and eat off-brand cereal.

7:30 a.m. – leave for school.

3:30 p.m. – return from school and do assigned chores.

6:00 p.m. – sit down at dinner, at your designated place; always pass your dishes to the left; take only one serving from each plate before passing it along; do NOT reach for anything without asking first.

Shortly after we moved in, I witnessed Robert jam a fork in the back of David's hand when he reached for a second pork chop without asking. Robert was particularly rough with David, routinely whacking his youngest son in the back of the head with his hairbrush. Robert stood 6' 2" with a tight, frizzy perm that added a few inches to his height. He probably weighed about 260 pounds, and those fingers that grasped that hairbrush were long and fat. He terrified me because he was so *much.* And he had complete control of my mother; he'd taken her away and made all these rules and punishments for disobedience that I didn't understand. Even though Dad had been scary in his drunken stupors, I could find relief when he was sober. With Robert, there was neither safety nor stability at any time. The days at home were shadows, and the nights were complete darkness.

After I absorbed the shock of Robert replacing my father, my entire life became a gaping void: only hard swallows, and feelings of paralysis in a silent tomb. That oppressive stillness was not solely the absence of noise. It was the absence of circulation. Understanding. Connection. Touch. Love. It felt like being locked in a soundproof room, trapped with the haunting loss of my previous life. I knew good things existed; I had memories of better days, but sometimes it seemed as if I'd never had them at all.

Robert claimed the adage, *Kids are meant to be seen and not heard*, which meant I could never express myself, as school was a controlled environment as well. I stuffed down each new experience, each new rule, each additional punishment. I wrestled my insides down into that dark, vulnerable place inside me I no longer dared access.

At night, I would ask question after question of my sister, Teresa, who slept in the bunk bed above me. I couldn't grasp the reasoning behind the new rules, and she helped me with another perspective that I could feel about things. She sighed in a way that told me she had given up a long time ago. "Just do as they say and don't mouth back."

"But what if I don't understand the rules?"

"Watch us. We already know the rules."

"What if I get in trouble?" Even *trouble* was new to me. It hadn't been a part of life before.

"You'll be okay."

But would I? Despite wanting to believe her, I wasn't so sure. This life felt like anything but okay. *Why was there not more food? Why did Mom have to live behind that closed bedroom door? Why could we not have soda?* Instead, Robert rinsed out a plastic gallon milk jug, added one Kool-Aid packet, and half a cup of sugar, but there was no separating the sour taste of the milk from the semi-sweet, watery Kool-Aid. Robert denied us treats like chips and sweets. Only on Friday nights were we able to indulge in popcorn, and sharing it with a tribe of other kids, with nasty hands, just took something out of it.

My thoughts consumed me with questions Teresa could not

answer for me. I was so overwhelmed by what was taking place, I couldn't properly absorb school as it'd all just become a haze. I don't remember celebrating birthdays, or even the slightest moments of reprieve. I only remember abuse. And moving.

We were constantly being transplanted across the country as Robert continually sought work in his field. No matter where we set up shop, the household remained just as bleak, whether we were in Small Town One or Small Town Two. Mom made the menu for the week after her Sunday night grocery trips according to what was on sale. I knew on Wednesdays if we were having meatballs, and if on Fridays we were having fish. We typically ate TV dinners on Tuesdays on those old metal top meal trays. We ate a lot of pasta and rice because it was a filling, cheap, quick fix for hungry kids.

We didn't get candies outside of Halloween, and even then Robert permitted us to have just one piece of candy per day. We had a trio of wooden canisters that lived on the kitchen counter. One had sugar and one had flour. Mom loved Hershey's Kisses, so she kept a canister to herself, and we could never eat her candy. One time, Robert broke tradition and permitted one canister to house miniature Tootsie Rolls, which we could not eat either. Robert took to counting the rolls when he was feeling especially cruel. During one count, two Tootsie Rolls were missing, and we all paid for it.

Like food, they similarly parsed items of clothing. We went to JC Penney's to purchase 14 shirts that were all the same style with varying-colored stripes. They allotted me seven shirts for one week and David would get the other seven, then we would swap our sets for the next week. Those shirts were a real treat, as we wore a lot of hand-me-downs. We didn't go out and do the big school clothes shopping thing. We didn't buy summer clothes, either. Summer clothes were winter clothes that were cut off at the shoulders and the knees.

Before the days of remote controls, all the kids sat on the floor of that trailer, acting as the channel changer for Robert. He would choose one of us to get up and press the buttons on his big old

1970's console television that dominated the room. I can still see him peering over the sea of children's heads from that velvet, burnt orange couch with the black pillows. That couch — along with its place in my memory — remained in the family for decades.

You, David. Change it to NBC.

Stand right there until the commercials are over, so I see what's on next.

Bobby, get up and find which channel Sanford and Son is on.

Find the news, Teresa. No, not that channel. Switch it. No, go back to the other one.

Jewels . . .

How I loathed the sound of my name when it rolled forth from Robert's mouth.

Although the house was stagnant, and we had no freedom to talk, move, think, or act without permission, Robert pampered Mom, which made us all feel resentful. Fridays — popcorn night — Robert popped a big batch on the stove. Mom would curl up in the corner of that orange couch with her own bowl with extra butter and a special little towel. All while the mess of us kids had to share one big bowl, feeling envious of how Mom perched like a queen on that orange couch.

Mom and Robert dictated every aspect of who we were and what we did. Our home life became exclusive; they permitted no outsiders inside. David and I always had to be together as they did not allow us to go out on our own. We could only occasionally ride our bikes around the block, delighting in that *ratatatatat* from the playing cards we inserted in the spokes. In more fortunate seasons, we set up lemonade stands to make pocket money.

We were just normal 1970's kids. If we went out at 10 a.m., we'd have to return by noon for lunch. We had that kind of freedom, but we didn't venture out much, because most of the people on the other side of our trailer park were a party group of adults. I never was comfortable being over there because they were loud and drinking. David always wanted to go over there because he used his mouth to get attention. Even if someone called him an idiot, he knew how to respond to get the attention of that cooler, older uncle figure. David was so hungry for love and attention, something I learned to recognize at my young age.

Robert abused David, but although David frustrated my mom, she would not hit him. I recall a time when she slammed the frying pan on the counter. But she would not touch him. Mom never really used physical violence, outside of irrationally backhanding me once, in anger. I forget what I'd said, but when those bony little fingers clad in rings clunked up against my mouth, I learned to keep my mouth closed. We were good kids caught up in an aggressive household.

As a two-income family, both Mom and Robert left for work early in the morning. They left the eldest kids to help the rest get ready for school, leaving Bobby in charge — a mistake. Bobby had to have known that his actions toward me were wrong. I wasn't even seven years old, and I sensed something was off. I wondered if people feel so stuck in the soupy mud of their own sickness that they feel incapable of making better choices. Bobby could have thrown off the mantle of incest and abuse he'd inherited. But he didn't. So, mornings before school became a rinse-and-repeat horror for me.

In the midst of always losing, I got comfort from Grover — who still lives with me today. He's quite matted now, yet like me, he is intact with all his parts in the right places. As a little person, I pressed my lips into his soft head as I rocked him, with tears running down my face, as I twisted his blue fur into tiny little dreadlocks. Eventually, I rubbed the color from Grover's plastic eyes — because I didn't want him to see. I filled his eyes in with a black marker. It was the least I could do.

David was only one month older than me, so he was old enough to grow suspicious when Bobby and I disappeared behind a closed door each morning before school. I protected David when he asked by telling him that everything was fine. Bobby was fine. I was fine. I became an adult for David, because I didn't want him to see what I endured. I couldn't rub out his eyes like I had done to Grover's. So I lied.

In keeping with the awful silence of my new family, I said nothing about the abuse. Going back to that space now and examining my innocence — I see the resilience of Little Me. I felt an inner expectation that I was going to adapt to the challenges in my life. I would prevail. It was my duty to help Mom, and the abuse came along with being a part of our new family. It was my cross to bear.

Innately, I knew that what was happening to me was wrong but I didn't have the words to express it. It felt like that terrible silence in the house; dark, cold, dirty. It was a *you have to go into the scary basement by yourself* type of feeling. I couldn't understand this shift in circumstances, because I didn't have that abuse dynamic with Dad. I was confused and sad. And no one noticed.

I went through the movements, but I was in my brain. Eventually, I learned to float out of my body and live above my consciousness. In the mornings, I would rise to the ceiling and watch the abuse. I didn't believe it was good or bad; it just was. When I grew older, I learned that dissociation is one symptom that abuse victims often experience. I didn't want to be in my body. I didn't want to look through my eyes and see Bobby's dark, greasy hair, green eyes, and crooked teeth, nor smell his rotting breath. It was easier to disconnect, so I wouldn't experience it happening.

I met a whole new side of me, a whole new existence. I thought these acts were a part of growing up. I knew that sexual energy felt bad, but I wondered if it was part of becoming human? Trauma is hard to make sense of. I did not ask questions of Teresa about my mornings with Bobby. She did not ask any of me either, even though she had to have known what he was doing to me.

Since I knew my mom was already going through enough as it was, I saw the abuse as a by-product of our survival. I was determined to not bring my troubles to her. Instead, I used my courage to protect myself, Mom, and David from the truth. It was a lot to endure and process; as a byproduct, I became a runner, in more ways than one. During mornings before school with Bobby, I trained myself to believe if I could hurry and suffer through it, I could get on with my day; which paved the pattern for pacing myself through pain for many years to come.

Those years were when I learned to manipulate to get my needs met. Of course, I didn't want to go into that space with Bobby. When he would oversleep, I sure as heck would not be the kid that woke him up. Instead, I busied myself with combing my hair and making crooked pigtails in front of the bathroom mirror. It was a small choice I could make to empower myself as I learned to move the pieces in my favor. I may not have had a lot of control over my environment, but I could hold what was mine whenever I found the opportunity. My strength reared its head when I realized that if I had to play by a certain set of rules, then I could choose not to be a dormant player. I would protect myself, a strength that would serve me well.

What happened inside the house and what happened outside the house were two different things. The person Robert was inside the house — the cold and domineering King of The Orange Couch — was vastly different to how he presented himself at parties and gatherings. At home we were whipping boys, but to outsiders we were his beloved kids. Robert never touched me at home, and if his fat fingers accidentally brushed against me, I felt repulsion. We didn't go out very often — hardly ever, really — but when we were in social settings Robert was full of affection for us. I wondered if anyone ever noticed how quiet we were: voiceless and propped up in the moment, like fragile, hollow dolls.

One time we took a family road trip vacation, piling into Robert's decked-out 1970's red van to tour around the Midwest. Mount Rushmore. Wall Drug. Mom gave spiral notebooks to David and me to paste our trinkets and miniature license plates emblazoned with our names. It was one of the few bonding experiences of my childhood. The moment felt surreal in some ways. I soaked it up like a sponge; in other ways, I was too skeptical to believe it was actually happening and too scared to absorb it. Despite being near my mom, I was keenly aware of the vast separation between us. No craft, nor decorated reality could glue us back together again, nor make the torn pieces fit. No snapshot in front of a historical landmark could rewrite our story, nor encapsulate a strained love.

I tucked my image of my mother away like a collector's item I could never unbox. She slept and spent her time in the front room of the trailer, while they confined me to my private hell at the opposite end of the hallway. If I cried out, no one heard — Grover, and possibly the god I always hoped existed, but was too afraid to put confidence in. In the mornings, we would come back out of our rooms at 7 a.m. and pretend everything was normal. But then when we had to go to bed, it again thrust me into a dark abyss where Mom would and could not be.

We only had one bathroom in the trailer. Mom stacked her small vials and bottles of Mary Kay makeup on the tiny shelves in the bathroom. One morning, I walked out of my bedroom to see her standing before the mirror in a slip, but she hadn't yet put on her skirt. I was utterly distraught. "What did he do to you?" I cried.

"What do you mean? What did *who* do to me?" Mom turned around, her mascara wand held high. "What are you talking about?"

In my experience, if a person was in their underwear, then somebody had done something to them. But despite looking quizzically at me, she didn't ask questions. She just shooed me away after glancing at her watch. "It's almost seven." And in Robert's household, 7:00 a.m. meant time to leave for school.

Despite my quiet acceptance of my new lot in life, I burned inside with an orange fire in the spot beneath my bellybutton. At the dinner table, over plates of meatloaf covered in ketchup or boxed macaroni and cheese, I felt a boiling heat in my belly at the surrounding women as opposed to hunger. *How did Mom not see what was happening to me? Why didn't Teresa ask why Bobby and I were alone each morning behind that closed door? How come my teachers didn't notice that discontent and restlessness that I wanted them to see?*

I was livid. Or at least I thought I was. Like many other things in my life, I disguised my rage. It wasn't exactly anger, but more of a deep pit of stormy sadness; a dark, chaotic well of emotions that drained my energy. The angry me was simultaneously the sad me, and the scared me. She was that little blonde girl with knobby knees, who desperately wanted her mother to wake her in the night and whisper, "We're going for a ride," to rescue her from reality. Just like she had before. Even then, I marveled at Mom's ability to be the hero and the villain of my life all at once.

She no longer whisked me away; she could hardly survive, nevermind saving herself and her child. We didn't talk about things at all anymore. There was no space for my feelings. And if I talked about things, she hurriedly shut me down, and I could not conclude. While conversations were not ongoing, that awful silence was. I felt myself blinded by the wrong reactivity, choking on begrudging agreements, and painful, covert contracts.

As I've grown into adulthood, I've wondered how I would react if I had been in my mother's shoes. I'd made an early choice that I would not have children. But I know in my heart that I can't imagine what I would have done to any man that threatened my daughter's mental or emotional safety. Granted, I'm a product of my generation, and my mother was a product of hers. I have to believe she made the best choice she could; and grieve the loss of everything she could not see.

CHAPTER THREE

⌐◝∧◞

Town Day

As a child, I loved Town Days. I snagged my spot in the front to watch the Queen and the Little Miss Coronations. I stood tall as the parade passed me by. The sound of the drums grew, matching the rhythm and beat of my little heart. There were races just for kids, and I learned that I could run. There were family comedy acts, music, and dancing. That year we were watching my uncle's demolition derby when Dad sidled up, a nervous smile sliding across his face. Dad took a knee before me and asked if I wanted to see his new truck, I nodded in that silent way that had become the new me. I was so excited to see him again and grasped his proffered hand as he led me to his truck. In a faster voice, he opened the door and asked me to get inside, then sprinted to the driver's side, jumped in, closed the door, and started the engine.

It was good; it was familiar, and it thrilled me to be sitting on that big bench seat with the aftermarket seat covers, just like in his old truck. I scooted over to Dad, just like I used to, with the stick shift on the floor in front of my knees. That's where I knew I sat. I could feel the heat of him next to me and smell that familiar cologne, and I relaxed into that childhood love space: this is my dad. But something was different. Even for him, he was very uneasy. I sensed a frailty — a desperation — about him, not the bark of dominance I knew from before. I recognized a similar fragility in myself; I wondered if I could champion us both by channeling the new bravery they had forced me to muster under extreme circumstances. I beamed quietly as far as my brightness would go, hoping it would cover him like the warm sun.

I am free.

Dad is free.

We are going for a ride to freedom.

I took a breath and let my back relax into a wonderland of safety. The soft space of my father's love, where I could be free of Robert's house; free from being just one in a clan of kids; free of Bobby and our mornings together before school. To my dismay, the passenger door swung open before we'd back out and Mom's voice said, "Jewels, come with me. Get out of the truck. Right now. That's right. Take my hand. Here, Jewels. Take my hand and step down. You saw your dad's truck and now it's time to get out." The pair had surrounded us — Robert pulled open Dad's door, as my mom began physically yanking on me while the men exchanged low, rumbling words.

As Mom pulled me away from the truck that smelled of my dad, he cried, "Please, don't take her from me again. Don't take her from me! All I want to do is see my daughter!" But Mom pulled me out of our sacred moment together just as quickly as she pulled me out of his life. My voice stuck inside of me in the dark part where I stuffed everything else. Mom and Robert led me away with my hand in each of theirs, appearing as though they were guardians, when they were only jailers.

I twisted my neck around in desperation, just to see him one last time. Dad bowed his head over his steering wheel as he cried. I saw one of his fists clench and rise before he punched the seat where I should have been sitting — and where I wanted to be sitting. Thoughts of the festival faded. The race, the queens, the parade, and the demolition derby were all forgotten. I tasted my rage at the unfairness in the blood pooling in my mouth. I bit my bottom lip too hard. No one noticed. I wiped away the blood with my sleeve, knowing it would leave a stain that wouldn't wash out for at least a month, and possibly a lifetime.

I didn't see my dad again until I was 18 years old. As I walked down the tiled hallway of the nursing home where I worked, I approached the solitary man waiting on a bench and wondered, *Is that my dad?* By then, years of Mom's statements crowded out my own in my head. Her vision of my father eclipsed my ability to see him as a person. Like an angry robot, I repeated what my mom had said to me over the years; I vilified him on behalf of someone who had single-handedly eroded the most precious years of my life. He was the only person who might have advocated for me, if only we had allowed him to do so.

"You're not my dad after what you did to my mom. I never want to see you again!" I said in her voice, not mine. I even stood like her, mimicking her body language that was far more expressive with him than with Robert. While I was no longer silent, I had not yet found my voice. I wouldn't for many years.

Shoulders hunched, as if expecting my rejection, my dad nodded quietly and prepared to take his leave. Sadness welled in his eyes as he held back tears; he kept his gaze to the floor. For a moment, I hesitated. I imagined calling him back to me. Telling him I didn't mean what I said. I was wrong, and I wanted to hear what he had to say. But I didn't do any of those things. My mother's narrative was too strong.

I later learned that after Mom took me away from him, Dad's drinking grew worse. He told me once that he sat in his reclining chair and drank for four days without relent. When he finally came to, he'd realized that he was a mess, both literally and figuratively. He knew he had to stop drinking — and did so, cold turkey. We definitely have willpower in our family once we make up our minds to take action. Dad remained sober for the last 22 years of his life. At least, he had that.

I can only imagine the patience it took to wait until I turned 18 so he could approach me. He had to play by the rules dictated by my mom, her mafioso lawyer, and Robert. He weathered eleven years without his only child. Perhaps he counted down each holiday.

Christmas.
Jewels' birthday.
Summer break.

Ten more years until I can see Jewels.
Nine more.
Eight more.

If his body language was any sign of how he felt hearing my mom's words parroted from my mouth, my rejection must have been crushing. That was the last I saw or heard from him until I reached out later in my life when I was two years from getting sober. It delighted him to hear from me and he pressed me to come home. I was so consumed by my disease by then that I told him that his small town was not my home, and I wouldn't be returning.

When we resumed our relationship, my sponsor advised me to take things at surface value, to see him for exactly who he was. I was told to treat him like the older man he was, which proved to be my coping tool. I could not mentally rationalize his existence, let alone connect with him as my biological father. I was in too much conflict about the ping pong years of my youth.

I'm grateful that we could reconnect when we were both in our sobriety. I saw a lot of myself in him, and I considered the notion that our addiction, like our trauma, was generational; maybe I could heal the generational pain in our family for good. Several years afterward, I set a reminder on my calendar for every Sunday to call Dad. As the phone would ring, I would feel butterflies of elation in my stomach, like I had when I was a little kid, the same way I had during our last pickup ride together. I'm so grateful for the years when I suited up, showed up, and made that phone call. When the first Sunday reminder popped up after his death, noting to call him, I felt such gratitude that in sobriety we had healed individually, and in unison. It felt providential somehow.

I was fortunate to have been able to see the completion of a lot of full circles. With some people, you plant seeds and hope to

God that something sprouts. During the years and the drinking, my father kept a light on in his heart for me. I got to know that; some people do not. When I went back home after he passed, I listened to his friends tell me how proud he was of me. I got to experience our relationship come full circle. My father fought with clenched fists in the pickup truck that day for me; knowing I would grow up far from him. He waited every day to show up for me, and he never stopped loving me.

We come into our lives with everything we need, but rarely realize it until we are on our healing paths. Our gifts can lie dormant for years, silent until we stir them awake; provoked to roar. Like too many, I had all the tools I needed as a little person but a sour cloak of other people's words, ignorance and willpower wrestled down my strength. My courage became an internal driving force, only rarely appearing; still driving my story but mute, even to me, most of the time.

I have a voice. I can speak for my father and me. I am certain my father loved me the way I loved him. I can pay tribute to the strength of a man whose life dealt him a rough deck of cards, but he found his way home. My father maintained sobriety for the last 22 years of his life. Now he will forever exist in these pages as a man who did his best.

CHAPTER FOUR

-⁻/\\⁻-

Westward Ho

We left our state in 1981 for the West Coast for Robert's newest job. We didn't have the money to hire movers or purchase plane tickets, which meant we had to drive all the way. Robert packed all of our belongings in a converted U-Haul for personal use. But by far, the best part of the move was that Bobby was now an adult — old enough to stay by himself.

Robert pulled away with our trailer while his son remained sitting on the curb with his elbows on his knees. Bobby was small and slender, shorter than his peers; and by anyone else's definition: small. But he had become my biggest haunt over our years together. As I studied him in the rearview mirror, from my cramped seat between Mom and Robert, I watched him grow smaller and smaller. A flame of righteous anger and hope ignited in my abdomen. My breath remained caught in my chest until I was certain he would not run after us or wave for us to come back and pick him up. Once he was absent from my view, I looked to the horizon to receive what lay ahead.

As our wheels feverishly devoured the highway miles with a roar, I felt an exhilaration I had never experienced rise within me. The air rushing through the open windows blew back the sand that had been my life, revealing not some broken thing, but a new me. I was no longer small and helpless, but reborn on those highways, as the pain of the past few years had gifted me with a fleet-footed evolution. The confusion, the angst, the dissociation of my mind from my body swirled around in the warm gusts of the Midwestern summer air.

Perhaps it was then that I felt the gentle tap of my spirit asking to move into the light of my power. It was best that I did not yet know the rough path that remained before me. But I would learn that all the pain I had encountered would serve a greater purpose. There is no life without the confrontation of pain, as pain teaches us how to receive. Hell, I was ten years old and was just happy to leave Bobby behind. But I caught a glimpse — a small one — of seeing myself as I knew I could if the world gave me the right opportunities. I was confident enough in my potential, and that with a little light, oxygen, and nourishment, I would be just fine. And in the beginning, I was right.

While we waited for the preparations for our house to be completed, we spent a glorious two weeks living in a tent in a KOA campground. The harsh rules tempered, it intoxicated David and me to run in the freedom of the outdoors. Our makeshift dining room wrapped around the fire, lined with tree stumps for each family member. Sure, we still had to pass the chow to the left and ask for permission for seconds, if there was enough. But the trees and the vast space and sounds of laughter filtering to us from the other campsites called to me like a beacon from the future I felt hope to have.

As usual, David and I ran together. We had fun! I could be a kid when I was around him as he was everything I was not — loud, funny, fearless, and brazen. He was so mouthy; it was as if his horribly crooked teeth were in disorder because of his mouthiness. Yet David gave me a living version of a different way to be, and I reveled in the not-me of David. Although physically David resembled Robert, because he was my age I could look past his appearance. That had not been the case with his two older brothers.

David and I ran around the campground, two little wildings

freed from the oppression of a brick-and-mortar home. There was a play area under the shade of old trees. A swimming pool with a lifeguard. Other kids who did not have to hide in a house after school and follow a routine of restricted living. We raced our bikes around the camp's paths, and I felt my voice prepare to rise from my chest. I did not yet bellow, but the urge was within me as I pedaled behind David, wanting to scream aloud in utter abandon.

After several weeks of true childhood bliss, we settled into our five-bedroom house on the West Coast. Everything was fresh, washed clean by the rains day after day. I met *tabula rasa*, as gone was the *by yourself alone in the dank, dark basement* feeling I'd experienced with Bobby. I didn't have the internal conflict of those mornings before school when the adults were absent. The household was safe with no dark closets or locked doors or dank spaces that cried of secrecy and nasty intent. Despite the rain, the little rays of sunshine were brighter than anything I had known before.

On the outside, as usual, we looked like a normal family. I no longer had the same-city conflict between my mom and my biological father. Despite his absence, his memory sometimes called to me, but mostly, he felt like a watercolor memory, formless and faint. In our old life, I had often overheard bits and pieces of conversations between Robert and Mom that were not for my ears. They discussed a certain desperateness about my father, and I just wanted to be far away from it. The first fingers of freedom tickled the back of my neck and I leaned back into that feeling. I'd felt love in my prior life, and this resembled it just enough. It didn't matter that it wasn't in full measure. It was a light rain after years of drought; and while it kept me oscillating between desperation and caution, I involuntarily absorbed it, and was grateful.

I could bring this into me.
I could be a new me.
I could know this longing is bigger than my pain.

Robert bought a used green Ford Maverick for Teresa, and once she got wheels, she was absent. I liked to watch her get ready in the mornings, singing as she curled her hair in front of that big old mirror she kept in her bedroom. Mom made friends with the couple and their daughter across the street, and a sense of community around us developed. Then Robert's oldest son, Thomas, got his underage girlfriend pregnant, and Robert and Mom approved them to move in until the baby was born. Despite them being given my room, I was more than okay because although Teresa had the major part of the basement, David and I each took one of the little side rooms and settled in like the inseparable partners in crime that we were.

We'd enjoyed ourselves for a while, perhaps too long; I suspected it was always too good to be true, and my feelings proved me right as Robert's rules reared their big, ugly heads. We didn't have money for after-school sports. And perhaps we didn't want the details of our home life leaking out; the abuse had to stay quiet. We couldn't afford any special care or notice, so we had to board that school bus for home as the school bell rang.

While the school bus dropped us off an hour-and-a-half before our parents arrived home from work, we were to sit on the stairs of the house until they arrived. Even if we had a bathroom emergency, or were sick, or thirsty, we could not go inside the home. Although Thomas and his girlfriend were inside, they wouldn't unlock the door for us. We were told to sit outside and wait for Robert or Mom to arrive home from work, and so we did.

By this point, I'd spent half my life in Robert's family with his broken children. I'd mostly forgotten my father, as the chaos of Robert's household replaced him. His rules and the missteps of his children became my reality and the imprint that would become my future. Although the lines of propriety blurred, inside that familiar loneliness chewed at me.

During a drive in our big old blue Impala that could seat many of us on the old bench seats, they placed me on Thomas's lap in the backseat. Mom and Robert were in the front while Thomas, me, and Teresa and David were in the back seat. Since my hand rested on Thomas's, I rubbed his pinky finger with my own. He bent my pinky — hard — and said, "Don't do that!"

I was confused. And stunned. I thought this was what I was supposed to do when seeking connection. I liked Thomas, and it felt comfortable and normal to seek him out. I wasn't yet aware that older males interpreted my actions as me desiring a sexual connection. But they had taught me that if I offered affection, then I would receive affection in return. I thought what I did was okay, but when Thomas nearly broke my finger, I retreated to that chilly space of my head, rubbing my finger while trying to make sense of what I had done wrong.

The abuse had stalled, but the vestiges of emotion remained within me. I was now learning about things such as appropriateness, propriety, and boundaries. But I had never witnessed them before, so they were hard to understand. I only knew that when someone else's sick compulsion devoured me, I felt numb; but when I stared into the eyes of rejection, I felt kicked in the stomach, and abandoned to my own internal wounds. It was confusing for a little person. If touch felt both good and bad—which was right?

When Thomas and his girlfriend had their son in 1981, they moved out and Mom announced she was pregnant with my youngest brother, Justin. Almost immediately, it was time to prepare for another move. Robert left before us to settle into the new place and the new factory. Mom stayed back to pack up our five-bedroom house. I can still see her in those terrible maternity clothes from the 1970s, inside one of those big, old white freezers, trying to defrost it, while her huge, pregnant body filled that cold space.

Robert returned to pack the U-Haul again. Teresa feathered off at this move, leaving David, me, and two-week-old Justin with our parents. Together, we all made the drive. The quartet who once lived in my first little town slipped deeper into my memory until I rarely thought of — or remembered — us at all. Robert formally adopted me, and I took his last name; they did not give me a choice.

Sometimes Mom looked at me, remarking that I had similar gestures as my father. She said that I reminded her of him, but her face was inscrutable. *What was my place in this reminder? A welcomed memory or a signal from a life she wanted to forget?* Eventually, I forgot what Dad smelled like. I couldn't recall the gravelly sound of his voice after a glass of whiskey, or how it felt to ride in his truck. His face became abstract, too. I forgot about those days reading books to Yogi in his doghouse. I replaced the memories as David and I raced around outside with our new dog, Turkey, that we'd found along the roadside.

Robert's brother, Richard, was the captain of a large fire department in our new state. He was a self-described big shot, a barrel-chested man who walked with the swagger of dominating a testosterone-fueled environment. Although he had a wife, a son, and a couple of daughters living with him in that big house, I overheard adult conversations about *mistresses*, my first glean into the world of infidelity.

Initially, there was a lot of excitement about the close location and our families spent a lot of time together. I, too, was excited about this expansion of family — at first. From the outside, Richard's clan living in that beautiful home gave us some street cred we'd been sorely lacking. Despite being the poor country cousins, at least we had one mark of royalty playing in our favor. My stepcousin, Shane, was about my age, and since I was a tomboy, I naturally fell in with the younger boys.

During one of the first times we spent the night at Richard and Allison's home, David, Shane, and I were in the TV room watching a show. After David fell asleep, Shane touched me in a way that I knew was wrong. I pretended to be asleep, hoping that he would stop. He was greasy-haired and gross, an overlooked and aggressive kid. Each time he tried to take down my pants, I turned to the side and pretended like I was sleeping, hoping he would leave me alone: that didn't work.

I didn't want Shane's attention. But when any male wanted to spend time with me, it wasn't the physical, sexual reaction that took place that I wanted; it was the feeling of being noticed. I sought that emotional connection to disrupt that awful silence of feeling absent. I wanted to know I was worth the attention paid to me.

Of course, I was aware of the other ways to get attention, and I could have easily taken another road. I broke the middle-school track record at my junior high school, for example. If Mom had taught me to concentrate on my gifts and strengths, and I'd had a family who supported my successes, I could have run track all the way through high school and college. I could have secured a scholarship and would probably be a doctor. I would have been someone else, with unique attributes to offer. Whether it would have been better or worse, I cannot say, as my suffering has yielded lessons that have been powerful and healing for myself and those around me. I have learned that because suffering is inevitable, we can use it for our good and change the world. Do I wish someone had protected the younger me? Yes. But I advocate for others like myself by protecting her now and writing about my experiences.

I came to an intersection at twelve — the threshold of puberty. Experience taught me that those dense and dark places, where attention happened, led to being noticed: I existed when someone desired me. I felt alive when the touch of another met my skin. They heard me when I spoke if desire was on the table between us. So, I chose not to carve an alternative path through those chaotic woods. I chose the road I knew. So what if the attention was on me as the object of somebody else's pleasure?

At twelve, I became biologically old enough to birth a child. I felt I was in the center of my personal power. My ego, personality, identity and physical appearance were defined. I felt strong. Powerful. Enough. Worthy. I accepted myself. But I didn't yet know that eventually I was going to have to disgorge all the *stuffed-down stuff* and transform it into a novel way of being; it couldn't just stay there, crawling around in the dark belly of my empty self.

CHAPTER FIVE

About Me For Me

When I was a little person, my dream was to be a nurse or a server to bring comfort to others. My God, I thought servers were fabulous. They loved you, served you, brought slices of pie, and asked if you were doing okay. And that's all my little heart ever wanted. I wanted to ask if others were okay, and I wanted to be asked if I was okay. Because no one ever asked, and I didn't know how I felt about things, I just kept peeling back old layers when I found the opportunity to do so, growing new skin over the scabs.

In 1985, I attended my sixth-grade graduation and Bobby moved back in with us. I cannot tell you if he slept on the couch. I cannot tell you how long he lived with us. He went out on a couple of dates and I stole glances at the girls he brought home. I appreciated how nice they were to me. But I reserved most of my appreciation for those girls having his attention and not me.

During summer vacation that year, I engaged in a game of Truth or Dare with some local kids. As we spun an empty Coke bottle in the center of the group, I knew exactly what I was up to; I was no victim of circumstance that time. I felt that burn of yellow fire down below from that center of female power. I felt powerful. I was enough. I was worthy. I accepted myself. I was vibrant.

Phillip was *fine,* and whenever he looked my way, my brain unleashed a brushfire of pheromones and norepinephrine that forged fresh paths throughout my body. It felt as if I had just woken from hibernation with a *years-long hunger.* Knowing I could feel want for a male unlocked another aspect of me. I didn't have to be on the receiving end; I, too, could take. When it was Phillip's turn, he didn't take a chance on spinning the bottle, but reached out with his hand and pointed straight to me. "Truth or dare, Jewels?"

I didn't hesitate.

Dare.

Phillip's move was exactly what I was hoping for. In a hopeful, brazen voice of a pubescent boy, he dared me to have sex with him. Although I was just twelve years old, experiencing the ability to give consent to what took place to my body birthed an all-new me. I could say yes with my mind, my mouth, and my body. I had a choice of yes or no. I could manipulate sex on my own terms. And so I gave my virginity to Phillip on my own terms.

After summer vacation, I learned that Robert's brother and his wife separated, and Allison eventually remarried. The divorce hit my step-cousin Shane pretty hard and when he got caught up in hard drugs, his parents made him an outcast. We remained in touch with Allison and it thrilled me when she awarded me a job at her local business. She also hired me to help clean her home. I was thrilled with that too, because the expense of makeup and tank tops and hair spray added up.

I was cleaning alone at Allison's house one afternoon while she was at work. Prince's "Let's Go Crazy" played on the radio as I danced around the dining room, using the mop handle as a partner. Allison had forbidden Shane from visiting her house because of his drug use. Likely thinking that nobody was at home and hoping for the opportunity to steal, he snuck in through the sliding glass door and found me in the dining room, mopping the floor.

When he came from behind me, I jumped, turning around in surprise and holding the mop in front of me like a shield. But I was no match for Shane's strength. He pushed me down on the three steps that led to the kitchen. Knocking over the bucket of dirty water, he dragged me onto the dining room floor and raped me.

It wasn't the same as those mornings before school with Bobby. I was older and mentally, physically, and emotionally aware of what was taking place. Pain is more intimate than anything else we experience, and so I refused to grant Shane permission to be intimate with me. And so it was with the smell of the nasty water of that spilled bucket in my nose, I felt gratitude that I'd chosen to give my virginity to Phillip that previous summer. I recalled the wonder in Phillip's blue eyes, and the way his lips felt on mine as I relived my earlier experience. By the time it was over, I realized again it was Shane on top of me.

Oh yeah, you.

Coincidentally, that very evening my mother announced that she wanted us to gather in the living room. On that orange couch we'd lugged from our other state, the lot of us listened as Webster, played by Emmanuel Lewis, described *That Uh-Oh Feeling* when he overheard a female student being molested by a substitute teacher. Since it was a TV show, he could go home and talk to his parents about what he'd heard. From them, Webster learned the difference between appropriate and inappropriate touch. I said nothing about my afternoon, even as it burned down there.

My face reddened and sweat stained my tee shirt as I desperately wished to be absent. Bobby sat next to me, so I concentrated hard on not looking at him. I hoped if I just sat still enough, perhaps I would be invisible. I sat straightforward and still as could be, angry at Webster. He described *That Uh-Oh Feeling*, calling me and my secret out before the entire family.

In retrospect, I realized that Mom asking us to sit down and watch that show together as a family was no accident. Mom and Robert didn't have the courage, and perhaps not even the words, to deliver the message as Webster did. But Webster was too late. I want to believe that Mom did not know, but we all feel that way,

49

don't we? All I could take in at the time was what I was feeling. The feelings, thoughts, and actions of others would have been more than I could handle.

After that, Robert seemed to go through some sort of phase, where he wanted to be more family oriented. He permitted us to redecorate the household and paint the walls in our bedrooms. After years of having exactly zero space to make a single decision for myself, given such a choice was overwhelming. I chose midnight blue and white for my room colors. Robert had no design sense either and painted this ungodly pattern of a blue wall and a white wall and then another blue wall and then white — with alternating colors for the floorboard at the bottom. He even painted my bedroom door white with blue trim for the insets.

He also wanted to teach us things such as how to change the brake pads on his 1948 Chevy. I wasn't interested in the task at hand, and most certainly didn't want to be anywhere around him, and neither did David; we were both terrified of him. But Robert would force David outside and beat on him whenever David made a mistake. David would get the butt end of the deal every time; that poor kid never had a chance.

From Webster, I learned that if you were being touched inappropriately, that you should tell a trusted adult. And when my world shifted — again — when Mom took a second job, I was plunged into a deeper level of chaos. Mom worked full time in a corporate setting and took a part-time job in the evenings at Kmart. Her absence in the home on those nights provided the opportunity for Robert to abuse me. Webster told us what was right and what was wrong. But what was I to do when Robert was a trusted adult and touched me in that *uh-oh* kind of way? I was scared and intimidated and grossed out because I didn't want him invading me even more.

Yet I remained silent, as always.

Some victims of abuse lament that their bodies respond to sexual acts. But for me, there was little connection between my mind and my body; I just went numb. I lived in my head and felt nothing below the neck during these acts. I thought of Phillip, the next album I wanted to buy, and the pink Dolfin shorts on sale at K-Mart. I could disassociate from my body that way. I didn't want to connect with my abusers in a sexual way, but intimacy is a part of connection and loving. And that's what I desperately wanted. Part of me wanted them to want to be with me. I wanted them to show me they were interested in me as a person. I didn't know that I had so much more to give aside than that.

The family unit obligation pushed me in directions where I didn't need to go. I'm grateful that I had that willpower during sobriety when they said — and I heard — that people, places, and things have to change. I took that to heart and could *snip, snip, snip, and snip* because it didn't feel good to be connected to Robert and his family. Once I was an adult, I didn't have to be a part of them. The whole family obligation thing didn't apply to me because they weren't mine. It would take years for me to gain my freedom, but little did I know that circumstances were already in play to catapult me into a new world. A new me was crowning, soon to be born.

Our regular babysitter, Sharon, lived one block behind us. When she first met us, she commented that we looked malnourished because we were so skinny and so pale. She constantly remarked that we looked ill. And we were. For example, since we didn't have dental insurance, we had no dental care. By the time we had an issue with our teeth, it was past the repair or preventative stage. The local dentist pulled our teeth when they rotted as there was no money for fillings, root canals, and certainly not for braces.

There was one time I spent the night in the hospital because I had a compound fracture on my index finger. David and I were screwing off like we always did when I fell on my finger and injured myself. Bobby drove me to the hospital, and that was the singular caring incident of individual attention from my childhood. I was always part of a pack, so to get that kind of attention was uncomfortable, and I didn't know how to deal with it. I still struggle with that today; that spotlight feeling. I don't do well with it. I want to shy away from it. I want to accept the praise, but I can't.

Perhaps it was because of Sharon's comments that Mom began searching the newspaper for a backup babysitter. That's how my mom found Michelle. It's funny how one disparate event can set into action an entirely new chain of events. Michelle was a single mom who worked at the YMCA, and ultimately had someone sponsor me to attend AM/FM camp — ABOUT ME FOR ME — over Thanksgiving break in 1986, my eighth-grade year. Providence had a hand in bringing me to that camp; it was the mother of all game-changers. Ordinarily, we didn't get to do anything after school. If it wasn't happening during school hours and paid for by the taxpayers, we didn't get to do it. We had too many kids and too little money.

When that big bus full of chattering teenage girls pulled into a fancier city for camp, my eyes grew wide at the glamorous area compared to where we lived. I stepped off that bus, a new me, determined to be one of the cool kids. They put me with a pack of girls from the other side of the tracks and once I started talking, I couldn't stop. I talked, and the girls listened and I felt like YES! I'VE ARRIVED! I'M BACK! But I had so much to say after my years of silence, that I just couldn't stop talking.

As I embarked into the unfamiliar territory of a listening and caring audience, I threw the silence aside like an old Frisbee. *Zoom!* No one told me to shut up. No one said I was stupid. They just listened with mouth agape and eyes wide. I was back in a space where I knew I'd always belonged, and it was wonderful. The adults were listening, and so surely it was no accident when the conversation nudged to the surface. The counselors asked me lots of questions, listening impassively to my answers. They praised me for any progress I made. I was a project and didn't even know it.

I was way too busy dancing in the attention 'cuz I was out of the drought. I just talked and talked. And talked. Years of experience poured out of my head and shot out of my mouth. I was a faucet with no handle. It was probably for the best that I didn't know that they require the YMCA counselors to report to the authorities the nature of the things I unveiled.

On the way home, one counselor, who was Michelle, told me I was going to spend the night at her house. I was still high on all the attention I'd received, and I didn't want camp to end so there was no argument from me there. It was like a beloved echo from my mother's whisper from so long ago: *We're going for a ride.* Somewhere inside, I already knew I was riding toward an entirely new kind of freedom.

It was dark when the bus pulled into the YMCA parking lot. As the kids streamed out from the bus, their parents greeted them with smiles and hugs. No one greeted me. Michelle took me to the office, and it was then that I realized that something didn't feel right. Robert didn't show; Mom arrived alone to pick me up.

Wordlessly, we filed into Michelle's office, where she and I sat on one side of the desk and Mom took a seat on the other side. Michelle asked Mom, "Do you know what's happened to your daughter? Do you know what's going to happen next?" Mom did not look surprised at the revelation that I had described sexual abuse at the hands of both her husband and her stepson. She did not rise to comfort me. She stayed on her side of the desk, prim, proper, silent, reserved. I remember thinking that I would have come around to comfort my child if our roles had been reversed.

Absent any emotional explosion, I went home with Michelle that evening, and Mom went home to Robert. Later that night, when I thought about Mom hearing my allegations leveled against Robert and Bobby, to the moment she left me in the care of another woman while she drove home to share a bed with my abuser, my brain felt funny. I have since learned that pain is a doorway to understanding, and Mom had to walk through it at her own pace, despite my judgment and expectations. Mom was so used to losing that that night's event was just another bad hand in her card game.

The next morning, a police officer knocked on Michelle's door, requesting to sit alone with me in the kitchen. He was too big for the little dining room chair, and his authority seemed to fill the tiny kitchen. I remember that he wore leather and badges and had a baton and a gun because I couldn't stop staring; I could not lift my eyes to meet his. In answer to his probing questions, I told him what had been going on at home with Robert and Bobby. The pipe burst at camp and I was powerless to stem the flow of ugly words. The years of abuse had become words that took their place in the world and reached the ears of the people who needed to hear them.

While I mentioned Robert and Bobby, I did not mention Shane. Although I was just a few years into double digits, I already realized it was best not to complicate matters by listing all of my abusers. Robert and Bobby were the two worst offenders from my perspective, and since they did the most harm, I identified them by name and actions.

Mom did not leave Robert when she found out that he had assaulted me. The police officer told me I could not go back to my house and live under the same roof as Robert, so Michelle offered me a place to stay with her — a lesser evil than going into foster-care. If I had entered the system, Mom might never have been able to get me back. Not that she deserved to have me back. Staying at Michelle's for a few months was a much softer way of handling the situation and seemed like an innocent choice.

But I was no longer an innocent girl.

The police officer went to advise my mom and Robert that he had filed a report alleging sexual assault at the hands of both Robert and Bobby. I came to learn that Robert called Bobby immediately to say, "Jewels is making up these stories about both of us." Although the authorities removed me from my home, the family unit of Robert, Mom, David, and Justin continued, functioning just like they usually did. So I set up in my new home. But this time it included smoking pot and drinking and sex with older men.

I became Michelle's free, live-in babysitter for her children as she was newly divorced and partying hard. But I didn't mind because I was somebody: the men made sure that I knew that. I think I grew ten years in maturity during those few months I spent with Michelle and her children. No one and nothing was off-limits for me; I was wide open, and all the surrounding adults encouraged my openness. I had no restrictions. Of course, it seemed like a good idea to sleep with Michelle's boyfriend. His name was Mike, and he was a construction worker, which meant he got off work at three o'clock every afternoon. Since Michelle worked at the YMCA, she got off at five o'clock, which provided a two-hour window for me and Mike to be alone.

I felt such excitement, not necessarily the byproduct of sex, but the straight-up thrill of somebody wanting to spend time with me. I remember that anticipation when I knew he would soon be arriving. Mike told me I was pretty, dedicating all of his attention to me during those afternoons. I was so hungry for the attention. When Michelle asked me if I'd had sex with Mike, I straight-faced lied and said, "No, I did not."

I already recognized how I could maneuver men while moving women out of my way. Women were my authorities, and I had to watch out for them because they were the game-changers. Mom was the game-changer of my leaving the house, and I was living with Michelle so she was a game-changer too. I moved the men around however I pleased, but in front of the women I knew to be proper and not show that secret side of myself to them. It was at Michelle's that I developed a suitable case of the fuck-its. I realized that if I can do all *this*; I don't need any of *that*. The fuck-its sprouted and grew in me.

Later, I learned I was not responsible for what happened when I was a kid, but I was responsible for what I did with it as an adult. That statement gave me so much power. I have decided that the seed that was planted in me will go no further. I am the one that stops the thread of abuse. There's a lot of power in knowing that I will abuse no one: I'm going to take it right to the grave.

CHAPTER SIX

—⁓⁓—

We Don't Need No Education

Mom did eventually decide to divorce Robert, and the pair made the plan to move back to our previous state in tandem so he could still see their son, Justin. Although I wasn't supposed to be around Robert, we caravanned across the country: Mom, Justin, and I drove in a Yugo, while Robert and David drove separately in his Suzuki Samurai.

Mom and Robert further stretched the rules when we stayed with a cousin of Robert's once we arrived. I was under the same roof as Robert once again, but David and I lived in the basement portion of the cousin's house. But that was a temporary stop because Mom would not be spending much more time with Robert. Soon David and Robert moved to one city, and Mom, Justin, and I moved in with a family member of Mom's nearby.

The changes happened fast. I started ninth grade. Mom became a single parent. I spiraled out of control. When you take a girl who's been manipulating and moving men around on the West Coast and drop her into a small town in the Midwest, it will not turn out well. In typical 1980's teenage fashion, I wore miniskirts and high heels, enjoying exposing the development of my body. The more traditionally dressed women hated me, and I used that to my advantage.

Our culture seems to be very good about not acknowledging

the silent conversation pre-teens are inevitably having. We fail children at this age, because we rarely talk about how they become sexual, as they are coming to understand themselves. It's like we want to turn a blind eye to their burgeoning sexuality, and to an extent, their identity. But that sexual energy becomes a part of us, as it's a normal process of development. It feels taboo as we think of pre-adults as innocent.

In 1986, I was navigating a world that really wasn't yet mine, but they had already plunged me into it without my permission, so I knew how to swim. It wasn't like I sought vices, but that was the group of kids I fit in with. I started doing drugs, drinking alcohol and dating older men: shape-shifting, manipulating, maneuvering. That was my vehicle to get where I wanted to go.

In the first quarter of that ninth grade, Mr. Frank pulled me into his counselor's office. He said, "We don't think you're going to be very successful here. There are other avenues to gain a high school diploma."

My eyes grew large as I processed what he'd just said. *What? I'm out of here? I'm only fourteen years old!*

Mr. Frank gave me the opportunity to drop out of school because he didn't think I would succeed at high school. Despite mentioning there were other avenues to get a high school diploma, he didn't bother to tell me what they were. Instead, when I agreed to leave, he said, "Thank you. And goodbye." So being a teenager with no support at home, I dropped out of ninth grade and I hit the streets hard. What else would you expect from a kid with no safety net?

I'm not sure it was even legal to encourage me to leave school, and I don't know what motivated Mr. Frank to request that I do so. I remember being flirty and promiscuous with the guys who were in the throes of puberty. I hung out at the smoker's corner and snuck off campus to go to the grocery store during lunch, but so did a lot of other kids. I may have been faster, but I wasn't the only wild kid. Not by a long shot.

I threw a party at Mom's little apartment while she was out and invited a group of kids who had also dropped out. Some were older, but we were all a group of druggies. It was Christmas time, so we took the stockings down that Mom had hung and irreverently put them on our feet and danced drunkenly around the living room, knocking over tables and knickknacks. We played Pink Floyd's "Another Brick in the Wall." When the line "we don't need no education" came on, we called the principal of the high school and our entire party drunkenly sang that song to him.

Mom was livid when she returned home to the mess of broken items, beer bottles, ashtrays, and dirty sheets. She was working three jobs because Robert was unemployed and not contributing to my or Justin's care, leaving *dropout me* with the run of the apartment. Despite Robert's earlier discipline, or perhaps despite it, I was too wild to be trusted with such freedom.

Aside from her full-time jobs, Mom always sold something on the side, whether it was Avon or Amera, a natural nail care created by a dentist. Mom had beautiful hands and nails, and since her hands were so elegant, she sold many products. She was always trying to find that perfect something that would get her rolling into business, but it just never worked out in her favor.

The court mandated Robert to provide health insurance for us and he didn't, and so when my brother Justin got in a very severe accident, Robert didn't have insurance to cover his care. Justin had torn his heel off in a three-wheeler accident and spent a week in the hospital, while the finance department pestered Mom, "How are you going to pay for this?" Since her three jobs didn't pay enough to cover Justin's hospital stay, Mom took him home and drove him to the appointments before the doctor did his rounds every morning.

Our home situation deteriorated quickly. Mom had become my enemy. I had some really harsh words with her because that's who I was at that point. She knew about the abuser, but she didn't take any ownership of what happened to me, or see me acting out as a by-product of the environment she had brought me into. Instead, she emanated an unspoken grudge against me as she had to work three jobs because she had to give up her husband and his paycheck. It was almost like I was at fault for breaking up the marriage. There was not a lot of support on my part toward her, nor her toward me.

When Mom moved to a new apartment, it had two bedrooms, one for her and one for Justin. I no longer had a place to call home. It hurt deeply, and I was livid. The way I saw it was that her choices were the root cause of my damage, yet she was not taking responsibility for the fallout. There was no offer of counseling or therapy or alternative school. Just a move to an apartment that did not have my name on it. She said, "Jewels, you have two options. You're going to foster care or you're going to live with your father."

My father?

She meant Robert, of course, because she'd severed all connections with my biological father. I didn't want to get caught up in the foster care system, and I knew I was way beyond the help a civilized home could provide. By then I knew I could manipulate men, so I chose the easier path and moved into the shack Robert and David called home. I could put my hand against the wall and feel the wind shake the place. Sure enough, the abuse stuff started coming up as that sexual energy permeated the house, as it always had. But I had a rage inside me, and I would not stand for it this time.

My brother and I lived in the basement, and since there were no windows, it was against the law to live there. In case of a fire, we wouldn't have been able to get out. But we lived down there anyway, because nobody cared about things like rules and propriety; Robert was happier than a clam that we were out of *his* space. He proudly entertained a circus of women, and the sausage fingers of that reincarnated sexual energy reached for my throat yet again.

I hated the conversation of having to ask, but there came a day when I needed tampons from the store. My mortification grew when I saw the box in his puffy hands: Super Tampons For Heavy Flow. I wanted to ask, "What are you thinking? I am fourteen years old! That isn't going in there!" But I was still searching for my voice, and I didn't want him to know about the private spaces of my body that he had grotesquely violated. No part of me wanted him to think of the only spaces of myself I had left, or that he had dominion over them.

I dated a few guys here and there, but there was no male protection for me at all at Robert's house. Men came in two packages: short-term pain, or long-term harm, and I lived for the highs in between. It was all I had to look forward to. I started working at an A&W Root Beer restaurant part time for pocket money. Then Robert said, "Your mom's not paying support for you, so I'm going to need some financial help. I'm buying more groceries now that you're here." I was practically alone as it was, and I was my only defender. And so, for the first time, I had a response.

Finally.

My voice.

I said, "I'm not paying you a penny! You stole my mother, my childhood, and my high school education. You can screw off." *Damn, that felt good.* I threw my stuff into a black garbage bag and moved in with one of my friends, Tammy, who had also dropped out of school.

I learned how to run when I was young, but at 17, I perfected the art of out-running anything and everything. I took a job at McDonald's and dated Jimmy, a drug dealer who lived in the upstairs apartment. When I moved in with Jimmy, his mom, her boyfriend, and nephew, I slept with Jimmy's brother. Then I started working at a cafe where I met Sue and Ted, and moved in with them. I went to prom with James while dating Ted's brother, Les, who lived in another city.

In 1989, I was nearly 18 years old when I started work in healthcare. This is where my father surfaced and I gave him the cold shoulder. The merry-go-round of men and moves started turning faster and faster. I could trust none of them, so it made sense to turn Dad away, too. The rest seemed to be some version of the same man with a different face and moniker.

Joel was a drummer in a band. We lived in the basement. We terminated a pregnancy together. The pace quickened with Ken, nicknamed Fingers because he spun records as a DJ. I lived with him and his roommate for a time. During my relationship with Ken, we went to a ski resort for a weekend and his brother joined us. He was dating a dancer, and I thought she was absolutely fabulous. She had all the slinky, sexy, cool clothes, made her own money, and lived on her own. I moved in with her and when she took me under her wing; I got in with her agency and started dancing at a dive bar. My life became a series of edgy outfits, sequin tops, and sexy stiletto pumps.

I was taking Medical Assistance classes when I met Kristy. I invited her to party with us one weekend and she started dating my boyfriend by the next week. I had the unenjoyable envy of seeing her in class with hickies on her neck. I hated her, but felt oddly ignited by the competition. There was a ferocious, egotistical rage inside me any time I was in the running for attention. Being on the losing end made me the perfect concoction of melancholic and malicious.

Traveling as a dancer was a big thing, as that's where the real money was. And so I naively took a traveling job at a bar in another state. I had maybe a hundred dollars in my pocket as I boarded a train while in the throes of my disease. I was feeling very glamorous. My ego told me I was hot shit — the beginning of every addiction, paired with the juxtaposing notion of, *I'll get it together . . . tomorrow.*

I arrived at the hotel, and it was a dive. In fact, the entire experience was as expected: terrible. The bar was the quintessential dark and seedy establishment that you see in the movies; the environment where the owner knew everybody. The crew was just me and one other lady. She was a seasoned dancer and was very secretive, so there was no camaraderie; we were just two girls trading off the pole. The owner scheduled me to be there for two weeks over Christmas and New Year's and I knew from the beginning that it would be a long two weeks.

Besides dancing, I had to sell drink tickets to get the customers to buy me drinks. They would pay full alcohol price, but the bartender would serve me plain soda. The agreed upon arrangement was that I was to be paid some minuscule percentage at the end which, not unexpectedly, was not the reality. Our dressing room was the kitchen, and since they turned the heat off, we used the stove for warmth while we hurriedly pulled off and on our various outfits.

When the owner of the bar offered to give me a ride back to the hotel one evening, I felt that *going in the basement* feeling rise within me. But I got in his truck and took small comfort because it was the same kind of truck my dad drove, the kind with the big bench seat. That had to be a good thing. It just had to be. And when the bar owner said that his friend was going to ride with us, I nodded because I'd shifted into; *I need to go with the flow because if I don't, I'm going to get hurt.*

In the cab's front were pockets to stow maps and other regular stuff, and while we were driving, I put my hand in one pocket. When I touched the cold metal, I asked, "Is this what I think it is?"

"Well, of course," he answered. "In my business, you always have to be safe."

I nodded again, because that's where I was in life. *Smile and nod. Read the room. Trust my instinct. Know the right decision. Weigh the consequences. Possibly make the right decision. Run like hell if you don't.*

"By the way, I need to stop at my place real quick," he said next.

I nodded, because that's the only choice a girl in my situation had. The three of us went upstairs to his apartment, the owner, me, and his friend, who was a Black man. Once he closed the door behind us, the owner suggested to me, "Why don't you have a seat?"

His friend turned on the TV and lit up a joint. While he smoked, he turned on some porn happening between a Black man and a white woman. I stopped nodding as my eyes widened and my breath caught in my chest. I had stepped into a play and I was the chief attraction. The owner of the bar placed the gun on the table. I saw it as the alternative for, *You're going to do what I want or face this threat on the table.* His friend sat down next to me on the couch, real close. "Do you want some?" he asked, offering me the joint. My nose flared at the stench of his sweat mixed with stale smoke.

"I'm fine," I answered, doing everything I could not to inhale so I could keep my wits about me.

"Can I get you a drink?" the owner asked.

I agreed. When he returned with something, I took small sips. *Was it spiked? Was I going to die? Would I be raped? Nobody cared about me. Would I even be missed? How long would it be before Mom noticed I no longer called her?* I continued sipping on the drink in a super alert mode until I thought my heart was going to explode out of my chest. Finally, I said, "You know what? I'm feeling burnt, man. I worked all night. I'm super tired. I want to make my way back to my place. Can we do this another night?"

The conversation got real heavy real quick when it became clear I would not be a willing participant to whatever the duo had planned. It got to where my rage was driving, just under the surface. When neither of them stood, I did, saying, "I have to go. I'm not into this. I'm not into whatever it is you're planning."

Thankfully, the bar owner dropped the idea of my participation in their plans, probably thinking he was supposed to get another week out of me. How would he find another dancer on such brief notice if he murdered me and threw my body in a dumpster in the next town? It may not have been much, but I had some currency. Without saying a word, he drove me back to the motel where I immediately called my mom. It was very early in the morning, and her voice was small. "Jewels?"

"Mom, you've got to get me out of here."

"Out of where?"

"I'm dancing at a bar in this small town. The bar's owner scares me. He has a gun. He seems dangerous. I need to get out of here right now, Mom."

As Mom gained her wits, she turned to the numbers. To the logistics where she was most comfortable. She said, "There are no airports nearby. You have no money. How do we do this?"

"I can see a little airport across the way. Please help me, Mom."

But there was no way we could or would work it out, and I had to stay the full two weeks. In the end, I paid more to that bar than I brought home. After that experience, I realized how many ways that situation could have gone wrong. I could have been the dead girl in the trash can, the stripper no one cared enough about to find the killer.

But these things didn't scare me. When I thought about what could have gone wrong, these experiences made me harder and increased my drive to succeed. I was determined to make more money. Money equated survival, and I could put a roof over my head. I had become the combination of all the worst characteristics of my parents. A vice addict, ensnared by the desire for a security I never had.

I started working at a club closer to home. I made a lot of money working four or five times a week. I rented a fantastic place in a prosperous part of the downtown area. I had a roommate, and I accumulated everything I could.

Money, money, money, money.

I didn't put it in a savings account or buy things. Nope, I stuffed it all in a box. It was mattress money. I didn't trust anybody; I couldn't trust anybody.

I was doing bikini shows where I met Jason, living with him for three years while I danced. When that went south, I dated different men and traveled to different places. I had my house club with a house mom, then I traveled on a circuit to work in little dive bars for the week, and make large amounts of money. Most of the time the bar owner would put me up in some sort of house where all the girls stayed, or I would stay with him. I met some courageous women who were single moms and stayed clean and sober; I met some women who started businesses and became successful. And then, of course, I met all the other ones who didn't do so well.

My alcohol tolerance ramped up significantly. I generally worked from four in the afternoon till two in the morning, and I was drinking the entire time. I started doing tequila shots when I first got on the stage, because I didn't want to hear what the men were saying to me. Alcohol was the supreme silencer of all the noise within and outside my head. When my superpower of dissociating from my life was not enough, there was always a sip of something stronger to take the edge off. By the end of each shift, I'd knocked back eight to ten drinks.

In 1995, my brother Justin severed his relationship with Robert, and they had their last parental visit. Justin wanted to change his last name to reflect that of a sports player he admired. Mom followed suit as they no longer wanted to be associated with Robert or his family. I was not part of that decision. I had swum too far out to sea, where I bobbed around, just keeping my head above water. I self-medicated at the irony that I'd had my entire childhood stolen by my mother's choice in men — all of whom she'd eventually leave — because I'd been right about them the entire time. The raw intuition of the young never lies, it's only as we age that we make things more contrived than they ought to be.

When Mom started dating Lloyd, I met his brother, Mark, who wanted to take care of me, so I damn well let him. Mom always said that knowledge was power, so I went back to school. I had gained a GED when I turned 18 and had then taken the extra courses to get my HSED. When I met Mark, we got an apartment together and the university to which I applied accepted me for pre-med. I realized that I was smart, and I was proud of my scores.

But in keeping with the turbulence of my life, my relationship with him soon grew rocky. During our relationship, he became increasingly physically dominant with me. At first, I brushed it off. But then he started showing up at my work and asking where I was. He would harass my coworkers, asking things like, "Where's Jewels? She said she was working a shift tonight."

When he left for a weekend softball tournament, I packed what I could in black trash bags. I put everything else in the garage, locked the door, and took the garage door opener so he couldn't get to my stuff before I moved it. As I left, I heard my mom's voice in my head, *we're going for a ride.* And just like in our first venture out to find safety, I was liberated, terrified, and completely alone.

I took an apartment in a historical building that used to be the old asylum in the city. When I walked down the hall to my unit, I passed the old windows with the slits that were once used to insert the food trays for the inmates. Mom gave or sold me her Ford probe, some furnishings, and together we created a beautiful little sanctuary for me. I didn't have a bedroom set, so I slept on the couch, but that didn't matter to me. Despite living in a former asylum, I was free, and I loved it, an irony not lost on me. I had my job in Behavioral Health, where I was growing in confidence. I was making my own money. I felt alive.

Mark and I had gotten two ferrets together, so he would leave constant messages on my answering machine that were always some version of, *Those ferrets are part mine and I deserve visitation.* Like Mom had done with Dad, I took out a restraining order. Then I met Mathew and moved in with him. When that ended, out came a new box of black garbage bags, and I moved into a townhome on my own.

I kept swimming, and I would eventually accumulate seven transcripts from all the different schools because no matter where I landed, I enrolled in college. I was continually working toward a nursing degree, but I never stayed put long enough to complete the coursework. Inevitably, I'd just take those credits and move to the next relationship.

Behind the curtain, I was drinking heavily; it was just what I did. I came home after work, started drinking, and logged into the chat rooms to escape the difficulties of my reality. I learned to tell elaborate stories and inflate my ego to become the carefree, successful student and healthcare worker. I could be anything they needed me to be, a skill I would hone into a razor-sharp success. My personas in the chat rooms were my chariots, escorting me from one relationship to the next. But it wasn't in the chat rooms where I meet and would fall in love with my first female.

A girl named Stacey came through the behavioral health floor where I was working. She was a cutter who had survived a terribly abusive upbringing, and she got hooked on her meds. I truly enjoyed working with her during her stay at the hospital. But there was something different about Stacey. She was silly, and a little flirty. And unlike any other patient I'd cared for, I felt a chemistry developing with her, an unfamiliar connection I hadn't experienced before. Something I would only ponder while in the shower, exhausted after a day's work at the hospital. *Why was she swirling around in my head?* I knew it was strictly against hospital policy for employees to develop relationships with patients. But I couldn't let the thoughts go.

On the day the doctor scheduled her to go home, I pressed a note with my phone number into her hand. You know, just in case she ever needed to talk to someone — knowing darn well I had great hopes that she would reach out for other reasons.

And she did.

We started dating once she left the facility. I'd been with women before, but Stacey was more of what I called a *boi*. She was so much fun to be around and truly made me laugh during our time together. We developed a safe intimacy, creating inside jokes that only the two of us knew. Stacey knew what it was like to be a girl, so there was no trying to explain the discomforts, as she knew firsthand. Stacey also understood my trauma as she had experienced something similar, and she held me in high regard with the recovery I'd accomplished, even at that adolescent stage. She knew what it felt like to be alone, unheard, and disregarded, and so we could hold that special space for each other.

As for the sexual side of our relationship, considering I'm bisexual, I would get very aroused being with her. Six months into our relationship, I came out to my mom as I wanted to invite Stacey over for Christmas. I took a welcomed break from men while I continued to attend school and work in the hospital. I felt alive. I was kicking. I was doing really well — if you were on the outside looking in.

When Stacey disclosed that she was transitioning to Adam, so did our sex life. Love is love, no matter what external things are put in place. But I came to feel that my plate was too full to weather the shift. I couldn't fathom the judgments of being out in public with her as she transitioned. Although I tried, I was not strong enough to weather Stacey becoming Adam. Being out in public as a same-sex couple was fraught with risk as it was. And mentally? I wasn't in a place to take that sort of criticism from the surrounding world.

Our breaks start with the smallest fracture. For me, it was when Mom moved to another state to help a friend and Adam left for a weekend softball tournament. I fell headlong into a deep depression. Although it was long in coming, it happened quickly. Everything I had been holding in all those years didn't bubble but catapulted to the surface. The grief. The abuse. My mother's absence. And now she'd left me, which is how I saw it.

When Adam left, I decided to take my life. I took a shower, shaved my legs, and put on my perfume. Because I worked in behavioral health, I knew how to overdose, so I cut my abuse bars in half and took half a pill every hour. In my psychotic mindset, throughout the course of a day, I kept over intoxicating to where my blood pressure dropped.

I was dead serious about my intent; it was not a cry for help. I didn't want anybody to show up. I was done. I was tired. But Source wasn't having that. Adam and I lived in a big building that had been refurbished into different units. We had an upstairs neighbor who was a friendly man who had been sober for a couple of decades, or so he explained as we met him in passing. Out of nowhere, he came down and knocked on my door. He was a fairly obese guy, so I wouldn't have pictured him to be my angel, but he was.

As I pulled the door open just enough to look up at his face, he asked, "Hey, what are you doing? You want to go to a movie or something?"

"No, I'm cool. I'm just hanging out." I planned to end the conversation and return to my death, but then in this little voice of hope, I asked, "But would you come in and sit with me for a little bit?"

He agreed and sat down on the couch. After a few minutes, he said, "You seem down."

I told him I was taking pills every half hour.

"So you are attempting to overdose?"

"Yes, I'm done. I can't do this anymore."

Calmly and lovingly, he said, "Well, Jewels, you have two choices, either A, we call 911 to get an ambulance, or B, you get in my car and I drive you to the hospital myself."

I chose B. He drove me to the hospital where they gave me charcoal and started the emergency treatment. In the ER, I said something to the medical professionals to show that I would not be safe on my own. The nurse let me know I was going to be staying with them and they charcoaled me and admitted me to the ICU because the CDC didn't know the levels when abuse-BuSpar was toxic.

Later than evening, an old crotchety psychiatrist sat at the table at the end of my bed, writing notes. I was restrained to the bed with leather restraints. Cords and cables connected me to the various machines monitoring my life's beeps and bumps.

The doctor asked, "Jewels, do you have anybody you can call? Any family? What about your mom?" So we called her and the doctor explained that I'd attempted to overdose and was going to be institutionalized.

Mom said, "I can't come back there. I just started a new job." I understood — as it always fell to me to do — but couldn't help but note that for Mom, it was always survival over me; and somehow her reality always inadvertently cost me something.

The next morning, they transferred me to the psych floor for a week's stay. They told me the rules for suicide watch such as I had to floss my teeth at the front desk so they could watch me not strangle myself. I had to wear a gown so I couldn't hide weapons of death. Truthfully, it was nice to be encased in those clouds of fluff and care. No one and nothing could hurt me there.

After a few days on the unit, Stacey-who-was-now-Adam was permitted to visit. Hy asked, "What can I bring you?"

I said one word: "Grover."

During my stay, I gained a bit of insight into not knowing

who I was. I did not know what my favorite song was. I couldn't identify my favorite color, or if I even had one. Yet I got my first glimpse that there is something inside called stillness. I realized I was not who I was out there in the world, but who I was in my soul.

I saw the molds and expectations of our human-selves. I glimpsed the minor roles we all labor in: getting an education, getting married, having babies, retirement, bragging about grandchildren, etc. Without realizing it, I had bought into the dogma that we expect women to look pretty and have husbands who support them. We expect men to detach from emotions and grind through to produce and provide for the family. We expect kids to be rude, moody, and inconvenient.

When my time in the psych ward was up. I walked home, carrying my white plastic belongings bag with Grover watching from the inside through his black eyes. I did not know who I was. But Source was tapping me on the shoulder and reminding me to question who I wasn't. I just wasn't ready to listen.

CHAPTER SEVEN

~/|\~

The Road to Sulphur Springs

The internet was my friend and my vehicle. After a few drinks, I sat down, logged in and let fate take me where it wished. Dating on the internet was a place where I could be whoever and whatever I wanted; a chameleon behind the screen. While the completion of school seemed so far away, I got my fix by being able to be whoever the person on the other side of the screen wanted me to be.

When I met Melissa on the internet, I moved to her city and started dancing again. I made a lot of money, so I got a boob job to fit my new role. But the incisions would not heal because of my escalating drug usage. The doctor removed the right side, but not the left. I took a job at Target because I couldn't very well dance with one boob, could I?

When I'd been dancing, I met a customer and later started dating him in his city, an Italian guy named James. He was the bad boy with long curly locks who hung out with an enormous group of rough Italian men. James loved cocaine. And when we moved into our first place together, he had one of those old combination Motorola flip phones with a walkie-talkie. His buddies would call and say, "Hey, I'm bringing over a housewarming gift." That meant they were bringing over an eight-ball so we would sit up all night and get high.

My world blurred as my more serious drug use escalated. It was almost like I wanted to function as an addict in the Hollywood way of doing it. On the outside, James and I looked like we had it all. We lived in a fancy apartment. We were young and beautiful with lots of friends. I drove a BMW that would eventually be repossessed because I couldn't pay the payments on a Target associate's salary. But except for that minor blip, I had arrived. I just knew it.

James's uncle owned a concrete business making curbs, driveways and sidewalks. James would come home with concrete all over his clothes — when he did work, which wasn't often. James also was the single father of a little boy, and anytime the mother dropped off the boy for weekend visitation, James would drive him straight to his own mother's house. Since he had no relationship with his son, I didn't either, and in my sober moments it bothered me a little. All too well I knew the feeling of being unwanted.

One weekend when James had visitation, I went to his Italian mother and said that I desired the opportunity to get to know the little boy. She agreed, so I took him to our house that weekend, but it was a total flop. Taking care of a child was not in line with the lifestyle we were leading. We weren't in the right mind to wake up early, manage feeding schedules, or provide attention. And so we allowed grandma to continue to have her power, and that baby was tossed all over the place to save James the trouble of being a father.

When my friend Jamie got married, she invited me to be in her wedding. James and I went up and how druggies always find each other, James found her husband, Craig. He was into drugs of all kinds, particularly painkillers. To celebrate his wedding, Craig had an open-door policy of free cocaine going on in his truck. So we would step out to *have a cigarette*, only we weren't having cigarettes — we were all doing lines in his truck where grandma and grandpa couldn't see.

On the floor of the passenger's side were five or six rolled-up twenty-dollar bills used as straws. I giggled and said, "Well, look at that. You're paying me to do your drugs!" I picked up all the little rolls and put them in my pocket, as I did my line of coke. No one noticed. Hey, it was free money.

At the reception, we had no need for food, of course. Our plates of filet mignon and garlicky mashed potatoes sat untouched. James set up lines on the back of a toilet in the men's restroom. In between frantic stints on the dance floor, we all rotated in and out of the restroom. Because both of us couldn't be in the bathroom at the same time because — morals — James would go do his number, then set up another line for me. When I did my number, I got busted doing rails on the back of a toilet seat by one uncle. Even in my fevered state, I could see in his eyes that despite my youth and clothing and beauty, he could see the depths where I dwelled. And it hurt.

Shortly after the wedding, Mom moved states and asked me to drive with her. The whole time, I was arguing with James on our matching Motorola flip phones. When I returned, the apartment where I'd lived with James was empty except for my two cats and two bowls of food and water. He had moved out. Done, gone, up and left. Without a word.

The quality of men I started dating circled the bottom of the barrel, joining the rest of my life. So many men, and I wouldn't know their names, but at the end of the party we were the last two (barely) standing. That was the currency I had to pay to keep going. One guy had a crazy nickname — Corn Nut. His bedroom was barely lit by a small lamp that illuminated a mattress on the floor and a few pieces of those old 1970's wood-looking plastic end tables. I had just fucked him. And then it was like I was seeing the room without being in the room.

There was a click, and then his lighter's flame gave just enough light for me to see the bent spoon and the crystal. He drew up the syringe, and with his arm tied off, slammed the needle into a vein. He quickly dropped everything on the table, untied his arm, and fell back onto the mattress with a *whomp* — which progressed to a seizure. My first and only thought was that I had just had unprotected sex with an IV drug user.

Then there were more names and places, followed by emotional and emotionless moves to different locales. *San Antonio. Ruthie. Bobbie. Peoria. Denise.* Each time I packed up the black garbage bags and made a run for it, my drinking escalated another notch, ramping up my tolerance for booze. I started drinking in the mornings. I lost all sense of responsibility. My credit score circled the drain, so I couldn't maintain a bank account or purchase anything on credit in my name. No one and nobody trusted me to swim to the surface for air.

But there was one group who loved and tolerated me.

I was drawn to people with fluid sexuality. One quality Source has given me is a non-biased view of others, which has always benefited me. I didn't have that something that held me back as in *I can't date that person* if I didn't have resistance against how they identified. I could go into a world where most women were afraid to go and happily hold that space for those with fluid sexuality. Having grown up in tiny, decaying rooms where my sexuality was used against me and could never healthfully flourish, I valued anyone who courageously took up space in their identity.

Walls had always confined me, if not the boundary infringements by those overpowering me. To see others harness their sexuality and cultivate freedom in that space made me feel liberated to relax into who I was. This made me approachable for those going through transition; they were grateful that I was the epiphany of a female who not only accepted their desire to be like me but also embraced, supported, and encouraged their transformation. I taught them how to do makeup and how to walk in heels. They valued me in a community that too many women considered taboo. It was a big deal to have people look up to me for simply being myself. I could do that, and hell, I even made it sparkle.

I wasn't sexually drawn to these partners; our relationships were more about the emotional satisfaction I got from them. A feeling of love. In the different varieties of lifestyles, we talk about being a soul lover and I think there's something very vulnerable about seeing people for who they are at their soul. I could relate to the stuff that was attractive to me, and to how they weren't accepted for the way they were, because that was my experience. No one accepted me for who I was. So I had fulfilled my wildest dreams — I was a server and a nurse: meeting others' needs, mending others' aches, and providing a salve for their personal pain when they longed for companionship.

I had these things in common with these guys and gals, which admittedly amounted to misery loves company; but it still felt like something more. Sexually, there wasn't much of that sort of exchange or dynamic. These arrangements were created out of love and bonding more than anything else, even if it was primarily trauma-bonding.

I got something out of these arrangements, which was my voice. When we went out, I assumed the position of the defender. I could speak up for them if somebody looked at them in a bad way. I had their back if we ran into trouble. Even now, there are haters out there, but back then if we had to stop to get gas, we were taking an enormous risk of running into somebody looking for trouble. Heaven forbid if we were to get pulled over by the authorities when they were fully dressed and glammed out and ready to go for the night.

In this new world, I could protect others in a way that I was never protected. I could preserve their soft, vulnerable right to exist safely. I eagerly and enthusiastically embraced this role, even though I was usually drunk. Still, this period of my life was the first time that I had experienced what it felt like to be the bigger person, and it was very empowering. I experienced a motherly instinct that I'd never felt before. I had a voice, and people listened to me, and they understood what I was talking about.

I stayed true to the trend for many years, being with the people who did not fit into the mold society put them into. If somebody was transitioning, cross dressing, or not living in their assigned roles, then I was happy to be there for them. I embraced this role with a fervor I had not felt before, as I'd always been curious about living in the mold, but could never conform. My mouth would get me in trouble. My actions would reap insuffer-able consequences. Alternatively, I never understood the point of fitting in. I determined it was all a big delusion, and most people were just fooling themselves out of having to live deliberately.

I stayed on the lower level of a friend's townhome: me, my be-longings, and my two cats. I was drinking heavily at that point; it kept my world ambiguous enough to forget. I only remember snippets from that time, like an old film on a projector screen; and all my memories taste like wine or hard liquor, and what re-mains still gives me a sour stomach. I got on the internet again — because that's how I got around — where I met Murphy, who was born as a female but identified as a male. I visited Murphy for nine months in hys city and my mental health deteriorated to psychosis because I no longer had access to the medications that I was on in my previous city.

Murphy wouldn't let me drink, so I had no way to escape the taunts of my unhinged thoughts. I called my previous psychia-trist and pleaded with her to call in prescriptions for me. But she wouldn't. She explained that if she wasn't seeing me, she wouldn't prescribe meds. I couldn't work in my mental and phys-ical state, so there was no money to travel to see her. So I went through a withdrawal process on my own, which was not only rough but dangerous as I detoxed from alcohol and my pre-scribed medications. But I was used to that kind of rough life, so I pushed ahead as I knew to do.

But it was difficult. It was not pretty.

During my detox from psych meds and alcohol, there was a time when my vision dimmed and I fainted. When I came to, I heard the shower running. I pulled myself up from the floor to tell Murphy what had just happened and he called the ambu-lance. Any mask that I may have been wearing to impress Mur-phy was now destroyed. It was only my darkness that showed now. I wasn't fooling anyone, including Murphy, who said, "Jew-els, you're a lost soul."

And I was.

I cleaned myself up over the next couple days. I started eating again, and the withdrawals from the psych meds eased. I was still emotionally unstable, but at least the fogginess in my brain dissipated and I could see straight.

But then I came smashing to yet another bottom. Two nights later, my emotions wore heavy — too heavy for me to break. I'd burnt all my bridges and there was no one left to call, so left to my own thoughts, I considered it best to end my life. I couldn't imagine enduring another minute of emotional anguish. I pulled on my coat and started for the front door.

Murphy, who was sitting on the couch, looked up and asked, "And . . . where are you going?"

"I'm going to go behind the trash dumpster. Find a broken beer bottle. Use it to cut my wrists."

"No, you're not. Come back here, take off your coat and go to bed."

I looked at hym, weighing my options. I felt no sincerity in hys voice, but more of a tired resignation. Hy might as well have said, "Not on my watch, little lady." But it was a little dose of love, and I slurped it up. I removed my coat and went to bed. The next morning, I awoke and kept trudging along.

Initially, Murphy and I were dating vanilla, but I noticed books and some funky toys on the top dresser. I became curious and asked questions. Murphy gave me the book *Screw the Roses, Send Me the Thorns: The Romance and Sexual Sorcery of Sadomasochism*, by Philip Miller and Molly Devon. I read through it and what initially appealed to me was that if I were a submissive, somebody such as Murphy was going to know where I was at all times.

He would have complete control over me. He would make my decisions for me. *Yay.* He would tell me what to eat and when I had to work, and that I could no longer drink in hys house. I would serve hym, which would mean that I was going to make hys breakfast in the morning and remove hys shoes when he arrived home from work in the evening. To me, that meant I would be valued to the nth degree. That's what brought me into the world. I had a lot of submissive qualities, and so the idea of that type of relationship appealed to me, at first. It was the love and attention I was thirsting for, and so for a time, we were a good fit. Even though the role of a submissive didn't fit, I had walked through the door.

My relationship with Murphy lasted for about nine months until I destroyed it with my behaviors. An untreated, dry alcoholic does not a good partner make. Back on the merry-go-round I went. Into the black garbage bags went my belongings. And via the internet, I landed a new fish, a counselor who gave me hope for a short time. Our relationship lasted until she could see right through me — which wasn't long given her profession — and I wasn't ready to be seen for who I was. Not by a long shot. And that's when I started drinking all day long. Life was becoming extremely uncomfortable, and I did what I could to numb out.

My pattern stayed the same. The only thing that changed were the names and the places. When my relationship with Murphy blew up, I met K.C. online, a Stone Butch who hailed from Sulfur Springs. In the depths of where I was swimming both mentally and physically, I stepped into my role as a femme. As did she: Prince Charming, coming to save the day. K.C. offered for me to live with her in her house and go back to school. So many promises unfurled from her tongue. I ate them up like those long-forbidden chocolates and Tootsie Rolls Robert had prohibited me from enjoying.

Making plans while chatting online, she'd said she would pick me up from the airport. Little did I know, K.C. would need to take a full Xanax to drive because of the anxiety she experienced in traffic. When she shared this information the morning of my arrival, I thought to myself, *Good God, what have I gotten myself into? Should I board the plane?* But what else was I to do? I had nowhere else to go.

When K.C. picked me up at the airport, she was about 20 or 30 pounds bigger than her picture — of course. She really wasn't all that masculine, but was shy in a feminine way. I remember thinking, *You're nothing like the butch I've been talking to online.* But to be honest, neither was I. And K.C. didn't ride a trusted white stallion; her truck was a two-by-two instead of a four-by-four. It was a little truck, which was going to be par for the course. K.C. carried my luggage to her truck and ushered me into the cab where a leather-scented candle was burning inside. Even the leather wasn't real.

Medicated K.C. navigated the traffic, and we headed towards Sulfur Springs. Both my physical and mental discomfort multiplied progressively with each passing moment. I didn't have the cash to indulge in drinks on the plane, so it'd been almost 12 hours since I could numb the uneasiness. Withdrawal sweat trickled from all the wrong places as I nervously engaged in conversation. My mind jumped from thought to thought as I hoped she would offer to pull over for a drink or five to ease our awkward chatter. But she didn't, and I wasn't ready to show myself yet. So I continued to twitch and fidget in that cramped leather-scented cab, praying for an end to the drive.

When we pulled up to her house, I saw it was the furthest thing from a house: a trailer home in a trailer court. The white skirting around the trailer's base was missing pieces, reminding me of a mouth absent a few teeth. A rickety staircase missing a step or two led from the driveway dirt to the aluminum covered front door. The sight of it brought me back in a flash to the trailer we lived in when Mom first married Robert. *What have I done?* With a desperate sense of resignation, I stepped out of the truck into my alternative world because I needed a drink.

Badly.

The inside of the trailer was no better. Kitchen cupboards hung from the wall at uneven angles. Some cabinet doors were missing, too. Upon closer inspection, I saw that there were little holes in the corners where the cabinets once met the wall but no longer did. K.C. watched my eyes and nervously offered that a previous girlfriend's rabbit had chewed at the baseboards. But all I could think about was that next drink, as I took the perfunctory tour of the trailer.

Steps down the long hallway, and into the master bedroom, brought me to the end of the trailer. Behind the shower curtain that tied back to each side was a bottomless tub, just to make the master bedroom super posh. Except the drain was missing. When I bent over to look down, I could see the ground beneath the trailer. I was literally circling the drain. K.C. chattered nervously, explaining each defect of the trailer as I rubbed the sweat on my palms against my thighs to keep myself from screaming, *Where is my drink?*

One thing, among many, that K.C. neglected to mention was that Sulfur Springs was in a dry county that prohibited the sale of any alcoholic beverages. Therefore, we'd make the drive to the next county to a drive thru liquor store where we'd stock up for the week — which meant I would have a lot of alcohol at my fingertips once we pulled that 2×2 truck back up to the trailer.

Despite the availability of alcohol during my sentence in Sulphur Springs, life did not magically improve, which was no surprise to anyone but me. We could barely put food on the table, dedicating our extra funds to alcohol, which made my waking moments tolerable. Yet I had a Coach purse and a big-screen TV, so I was okay. In my addled mind, I was living a luxurious life. In reality, I was living in a trailer house valued at $1,300 — but I was determined to make it home. I was so used to making the best out of what I had, that I felt it was my only option. It's hard to note the slippage when you're drinking as heavily as I was.

Despite my flaws, I am not a stupid woman, though I admit to delving into the delusional in Sulphur Springs. I mixed Slim-Fast with my vodka in the mornings. I read the container and thought, *Just look at all those vitamins! I'm going to remain healthy as the vitamins will serve my body and the vodka will numb it, keeping me safe and free from harm.*

As crazy as this sounds, my ego was my ride or die that kept me in check. If it weren't for that powerful force, I may have settled for the many less-than situations before. My looks and my figure kept me moving because I figured that as long as I could stay skinny and semi-attractive, I could wiggle my way out of any situation gone bad.

As the race to the bottom of the drain progressed, I started taking pills. I thought that since I was feeling anxious, perhaps K.C.'s meds would help take the edge off. However, I didn't know that the protocol was to take little pieces of Xanax, so I swallowed an entire pill. *There's nothing going on today, so I might as well take this pill.* Terrible decision. That was the first time I ever blacked out from drugs — I lost a full 24 hours of my life.

K.C. was a teacher, so when September rolled around, she went back to school during the day and I took a job at Walmart. The first day I showed up, I was a little tardy because I didn't yet know where I was going. Or maybe my hair wasn't perfect enough. Who knows? When I walked in for my first day of training, I faced a very large Black woman with that kind of outright Southern personality that always terrified me. I wriggled in and apologized for being late.

"You one of those damn Yankees, aren't you?" she asked, fixing me with her glare.

Now, Black women already intimidated me, in fact they scared the living hell out of me. Just being in the same room as a strong Black woman made me nervous, as it was the antithesis of everything I understood a woman could be. So, when the trainer made a comment that I didn't even understand, I just shrunk. Was a Yankee good or bad? I didn't know. But when you preface it with the word "damn," it couldn't be a good thing. It had to mean that I was different, and that I was not one of them.

But Walmart was the only place I could work; the only place that would hire me. I needed money to feed my addiction, so I pushed forward despite not fitting in. I soon learned that I really wasn't different from the other employees as they were about my age at the time and had accomplished the same as I had up to this point, which wasn't much. We were all living paycheck to paycheck, feeding our addictions. Beer. Food. Xanax. Sex. Vodka.

I had reached the end of experiencing that horrible feeling of slinking into a bank to open a checking account. Too many times I sat on the other side of a desk, waiting for the credit check to reveal my instability and irresponsibility. There arrived the day when I no longer qualified for a checking or savings account. The repo of the BMW and the outstanding dues from broken apartment leases wreaked havoc on my credit report. Yet I'd hold my breath, knowing darn well that chances were slim to none of being approved. I felt so worthless, withering before the eyes of the representative who delivered the NO.

Mom offered to share her bank account with me. Walmart directly deposited my checks into her checking account, and she provided me with a debit card to access the money. I was 34 years old, sharing a cellular phone plan and bank account with Mom, which was probably the only way she could stay connected with me.

When Mom visited with her French manicured toes and fingernails and perfect haircut, I could practically hear her heart drop. K.C. had gone to great lengths to prepare for Mom's visit. She'd cleaned out the spare room that was used for storage. She'd washed the bedding, vacuumed the floor, and even put a little bouquet of freshly picked weeds by Mom's bedside. She buffed and shined that sad little place up with anticipation of meeting her future mother-in-law. But as we drove into our parking spot in front of the trailer, I could feel Mom's horror.

As soon as she could, Mom pulled me aside and whispered, "Are you kidding me? Jewels, this is not right!"

"What's not right?"

"Nothing! Not this lifestyle. Not this trailer. Not this location. Not this partner."

"Mom, this is perfect," I said, because, well, delusional.

She repeated, "No, this is not right." And although she stayed for the originally planned ten-day visit, her presence put a great strain on the three of us. We were all hiding our true selves and pretending. Mom got to see, firsthand, how I was really living. When we visited K.C.'s relatives, K.C. got wild and threw a hat at my mom in anger before the group. That was probably the last straw.

I had some delusional pinnacle in mind as I'd played out my days in Sulphur Springs. Wake. Add vodka to SlimFast. Down it. Work at Walmart. Keep the facade going. Yet I believed that if I could be good enough at whatever that was, I would arrive. If I had enough money and therefore security, which for me meant safety, then I wouldn't have to rely on anybody else — a value deeply ingrained by my mom's life with Robert.

Mom left, and the glue that held me together melted immediately. I paid a soul tax for hiding my true self and while I'd held it together for ten days, shortly after Mom left, the match met the dynamite inside me. There was a tremendous explosion between K.C. and I. See, K.C. was a stone butch. She enjoyed her femme girlfriends to be just that . . . feminine. And when I wasn't prancing around in the house in high-heeled shoes like she expected, she became upset.

Mom had struggled enough in her own life, and she hoped that I would marry wealthy. She made it abundantly clear to me that this was certainly not going to happen with K.C. If Mom didn't fully support me, then I had the chance of losing her love and attention, which I couldn't bear.

The penultimate explosion between K.C. and me blew me down a back road in Sulfur Springs with my Coach purse over my shoulder, a blanket knitted by Mom, Grover, and my two cats in their carrier. I had absolutely no idea where I was going, but I knew damn well that it was time to get out of there.

"We're going for a ride," Mom said when I called. *We're always going for a goddamn ride.* She flew a friend's two sons into Dallas to pick up a U-Haul truck and drive to Sulfur Springs. They packed up my big-screen TV because I sure as shit wasn't leaving without it. I put my two cats in the back of the truck because one guy was allergic to them, filled a Gatorade bottle full of box wine, and we sped out at first light. I'd already started drinking for the day and was nice and drunk as the sun shone the first rays across the sky.

CHAPTER EIGHT

The Last Swallow

As usual, Mom picked me up and brushed me off, telling me that everything was going to be fine. She said she couldn't help me out financially, but was sure we could figure out something. Although her apartment was small, she made room for me and my two cats. Despite being 34, I was happy to sleep on my mom's red couch, like royalty. The delusion of alcoholism was real.

I wonder how Mom felt about seeing what I had become. Did she take responsibility in her mind? Did she think I was just naturally flawed? She was as inexplicable as always, so whatever she thought, she kept it to herself.

I started working with her as the front receptionist during tax season. They paid me under the table and I saved all my money, got back on medication, and continued to drink. Life was normal again, which meant I was raring to go back online. My vehicle was sex; it got me everywhere I wanted to go, quickly, and helped me score my next scenario, which was even more glamorous than any of my previous scenarios. Enter Daniel, a business owner by day, father by night, and cross-dresser — Dani — by the weekend.

I had arrived once again. No longer a Sulphur Springs back 40 drinker, I was on the West Coast, drinking and partying with all the girls, including Daniel, who was a very successful makeup artist. He did the makeup for some very popular movies. So many famous people and giants in the entertainment industry surrounded me. I'd hit the jackpot.

Daniel moved his ex-wife out of the front office and put me there, even though I didn't know what I was doing. He thought I was the best thing since peanut butter and jelly because I accepted him and his cross-dressing ways, so I could write my own script. We continued using and partying even though he had an eight-year-old son that lived with him. There was no grandma in the picture to take that little boy, so he was stuck with us. I stayed with Daniel until I ultimately made a disaster of that relationship. The sun set on my days in there as I hauled my black garbage bags to the Midwest.

When I was drinking, I thought it was the answer to feeling invisible. Yet I was always chasing the idea that one day I was going to be seen. I was going to be a normal person. I was always trying to fit or figure or conform. But I could never find that Rubik's cube type of fit. I would feel so close, but I could never lock it in. So I kept shifting from relationship to relationship, constantly seeking that sort of fit. After each relationship imploded, out came me, the black garbage bags, and Grover — with his black eyes, just like mine.

The trauma and abuse was an enormous block that hadn't healed yet. My entire life's existence effort continued to move from person to person and from situation to situation. That's when the chisel of hope chipped away at the question of, *Am I ever going to find it?* Psychologically and spiritually, I found my real bottom.

I took a job working the night shift in the adolescent wing of a private pay behavioral health hospital so I could use my friend's car while she slept. It wasn't long before I was back on the computer to meet more gay women. Cue Steph, a very butch woman. Naturally, the talk soon turned — let's be honest, I orchestrated it — into a move. I came down on Thanksgiving in 2006 for a "visit" and me and the garbage bags moved in with

Steph.

A hospital hired me, located close to where I lived with Steph. You may have heard that alcoholics live two lives. My resume reflected great skill in healthcare, and I could draw attention. Once hired, I would eagerly accept any position in order to become an employee. After a few weeks, I'd start asking around the different floors for openings. I was very enthusiastic and would gratefully accept open shifts as a floater. It was a win/win: I loved the extra money, and they loved the extra coverage.

Steph had a kegerator in the kitchen. Now I was never a big beer drinker because I was much higher class than that. I was shaking martinis and drinking sake, probably with a koozie around them, having dropped the SlimFast. Steph's kegerator was basically a college mini refrigerator with a keg inside and a spout on the top. Yep, Steph had a tapper right there in our kitchen for convenience. But it was logical because it's much cheaper to buy a keg than it would be to buy cases of beer.

So, Steph had it all: the kegerator, the fire ring, the truck, the house, and a drain in her bathtub. Steph had the whole setup in Fort Worth that in my deluded mind felt like the answer to everything. She could take care of me because she had *the things*. But Steph's role in my life was a vehicle that drove me to her friends, Jennifer and Alicia.

On occasional weekends, we would visit and spend the night because of the distance between our homes. I got to know them well enough to be slightly comfortable, but I didn't vibe with them. Steph worked as a grip in video and audio, and during the off season, she worked as a valet at a hotel. While Steph was working on March 29, 2007, I hung with Alicia and Jennifer with plans for the three of us to meet Steph after her shift.

As we waited, I was in the back of their Chevy Blazer when I said something like, "I just wish I didn't drink so much." It was an effortless and fleeting thought; a burp from rock bottom. Unbeknownst to me, the radars of my two angels in the front seat of that truck went up. I didn't know that Jennifer was in recovery for pills and Alicia was in Al-Anon. As I mentioned, I didn't really vibe with them all that well, which only made their impact on my life even more remarkable. I've learned that we don't choose our angels.

Until that very moment when those careless words fell from my mouth, I had been trying with that deep hope to say one more thing or do one more thing and get it right. I can't say the hope was gone because that would be death; there's always hope until that point. But the effort wasn't there anymore. I was losing steam on accessing that shift, on pulling the lever of the hypothetical hatch that would allow me to climb out of my life and into fully living.

Within 30 minutes of my accidental utterance, Alicia had figured out where the nearest AA meeting would be. Jennifer was on her phone with her mom asking her to meet us at a meeting. They knew they had a live one; although I was pretty oblivious as to the sequence of events that was unfolding around me. As soon as those words fell from my mouth, it was happening. This huge energy tornado of action was taking place. In the front seat, the wave passed. "You will not tell us no. You're going to this meeting."

Finally. Something good was taking me, and I was not navigating. The two people in the front seat didn't know me, but they cared about me even when I couldn't and didn't care about myself. Overwhelmed with myself, I agreed to go to the meeting. Something wrestled my ego into the floorboard of the back seat and I shut my mouth.

Thirty minutes later, I found myself in the rooms of AA. Now I was the *Martini Girl* and that *Damn Yankee*, and when I walked in that room, my very first thought was, *Well, this is just gross.* Back then, you could still smoke in the rooms, so there was the smoker's room encased in glass. The walls were yellow; the ceilings lined with black stains; the furniture had ash marks on it. Every time a door opened, a potent stench would roll out. So we headed to the nonsmoker's room and stepped through a sea of legs of what had to have been sixty people in there.

But I sat down with Jennifer on one side and Alicia on the

other, and Jennifer's mom was there, too. *What is this? A therapy thing? Is this real? Where am I? What am I feeling? These aren't my people, but my God, these are my people.* I felt that common thread of love between all who gathered together in the name of addiction. When the leader asked if there were any newcomers, Alicia whispered that I had to raise my hand. I proudly did so, not understanding what it meant to be a newcomer.

I felt numb, but took those first halting steps into my heart. I was inside of myself for the first time in a very long time. I wasn't floating above. I wasn't medicated. I wasn't drunk. I was inside Jewels, the person I'd been running from for far too long. I felt a lot of sadness, but not out in the room. Only where I was sitting. Inside me. On the Island of Jewels.

I started crying and couldn't stop for the duration of the meeting. I could feel the love in the room, but my mind wouldn't let me connect with it just yet. It was way too foreign. I didn't know any of those people, and they really didn't look like me, yet I felt the embrace of belonging. In my mind, I imagined that I could feel and see the redness of my heart tissues. That's how deeply I explored myself. My abandoned house welcomed me home.

The group passed an envelope around that I still have, and the ladies scribbled their phone numbers on the back. After the meeting, I got my first chip, and they handed me that envelope filled with pamphlets that I still have today: my first token of hope.

Afterward, Alicia said, "Let's find you another meeting."

And so it was that the same drive that pushed me through the catastrophes of my disease became the drive that saved my life. The persistent nature of my addiction became the push that would get me from one meeting to the next. I found a group the next day. I was told to call, and someone would answer the phone and give me directions.

The guy who answered the phone was a crotchety old man. When I heard his voice, I thought maybe it wasn't a good idea for me to go, but my intuition insisted that I go to that meeting, no matter what. That old crotchety man stayed in my life for quite a few years thereafter. He was the one who greeted me when I walked in that door of my home group. And he continued to accept me for those next nine months when I was the most intolerable person in the room.

I was angry. Unbearably angry. Unapologetically angry. I had had enough, and those people were going to listen to me. Everything I had been drinking down came up with a vengeance when I stopped using alcohol to quiet my inner rage. I was healing.

This time, I had arrived.

CHAPTER NINE

Angry Antennae

When I finally stripped the past away to start anew, I was all I had; I was the steward of my soul. There was no one left in my life, save my mother, and I would soon lose her, too. I had moved many times and burned every bridge in my wake. I didn't stay in the same place for very long, primarily because staying was never an option: *Take your black garbage bags and get the hell outta here!* I was a runner, and since I ran; I didn't have a safe place to call home. So I sprinted downhill, quick and easy as the idea of a warm house with the porch light still on just for me slipped out of reach.

Sobriety was an overwhelming wave pulling me into that healing space, one I didn't know existed. Even though it didn't fit in the beginning, recovery was like a stiff fresh pair of shoes that would take time to wear in. It gave me hope, which was what my soul thirsted for. I crawled among the other people in the rooms on my hands and knees through the tunnel of refinement from my old life to new. I knew I was a phoenix; it would just take time for me to rise from the death I was leaving behind.

I wanted to feel my emotions in a way that neither consumed nor controlled me. The anger I felt was so white hot, I felt it coursing through my body all the time. It scared me; and kept me throttling toward destruction, even when I pressed it down.

I refused to let the rage rising to the surface destroy me. So, I pushed it outward onto everybody else, and recognized a thematic:

You can't tell me what I need to do!

Once, someone suggested that I not wear my favorite *revealing clothing*. They suggested I *might want to cover up*. The blood rose to the top of my head, as I experienced a blackout, dizzying rage. *Oh, hell no! I was going to be ME. I would no longer hide myself to accommodate others.* Instead of shrinking, as I would have done in the past, I sat up tall and straight and said, "Well, maybe other people need to know how to deal with the reality of bellies and boobs. Humans are made of skin covered bodies. Why should I have to cover mine to make somebody else feel comfortable?"

Whew, that felt damn good!

I worked 12-hour shifts at the hospital from seven to seven. My home group meeting started at seven p.m., but I was determined to sit in that room; it was my right and my privilege to arrive at 7:20 p.m., if that's what I had to do. Something kept me going to the room no matter what. And no matter what I wore. It was the only place where I felt understood because I had earned my chair, my seat in those rooms.

I rubbed each new coin I earned between my fingers and felt the reality of the Serenity Prayer as I struggled to memorize it. As I drove to and from those first couple of meetings, I said aloud, "God, grant me the ... grant me ... grant me that thing. I hope for this thing and the wisdom to do the best." In the beginning I had no clue how to move forward, but I just kept showing up. I had nowhere else to go.

I landed in those rooms because the gift of desperation was mine. I didn't have access to treatment centers. I didn't receive help from my family. I didn't have anyone or anything to lean on: my survival came down to me and Source. I learned in the room that there's only so much one person can do for another. It all comes down to you. You gotta want it. You gotta do the work. All the family in the world can't save you. So, like everybody else in the rooms, I arrived alone.

At 7:20 p.m. each evening, I could be that complete misfit, that one hundred percent raging woman. I didn't always feel like the brawny warrior I was; cultivating confidence took time. Yet the people in the rooms rooted for me every step of the way. There were so many years' worth of buildup that I just kept exploding, unleashing unbridled emotion, vomiting up truths I'd kept buried since I could speak. To sit in that room and let that stuff I was carrying around roll out of my mouth was such a relief. During the upheaval process, there were sprinkles of other things happening, such as learning about the 12 Steps, and considering who might become my sponsor, but primarily I spent my time unloading. I wasn't exactly ready to immerse fully, and that was okay too, which was refreshing.

I had to edge into the concept of surrendering to a power higher than myself. I could admit I was powerless, hell — look at my life, so that was easy. But handing my mess over to a separate entity? All the powerful people in my life had only ever failed me, so what would *surrender* get me? After feeling victimized my entire life, and *surrendering* every part of my body and soul to many violations, I learned to look beyond the words and the semantics of the program to language that worked for me. Especially because God, in Western society, is most commonly attributed with male characteristics, that, in no way, felt safe.

I had to re-define the words I was learning in their language to something I could stomach. I was so raw that I had to take it in slowly, filtering every word, lest I overwhelm myself. For example, I was okay with the concept of handing something over, but the word *surrender* was too much of a stretch for me. I could use *unmanageability* as a substitute word for what wasn't working in my life, but that's as far as I could adopt the language at the beginning.

As my attendance in the rooms became more consistent, I familiarized myself with the folks who had maintained decades of sobriety. They were actual royalty, these ancient sober Buddhas, and I fell at their feet, an angry neophyte, intent on staking my place in the program. At first, I believed they were so beyond me that I struggled to have a conversation with them. I was still delusional, and I thought they had all these extra levels of sobriety and that somehow made them different from me.

One of my profound times in the room was when this guy shared and absolutely charmed me. A Buddha with ten years of sobriety; he was one of the grandiose folks I worshipped. Well, I decided it was appropriate for me to share right after he did. I introduced myself, and as I started sharing, the Buddha stood and walked out of the room. I panicked, shooting a humiliated glance at his back. *What?! Don't you want to hear what I have to say?* He was probably going to the restroom or refilling his coffee, but that's how easily-triggered I was in the beginning — anyone or anything could set me off.

In AA, I learned a common saying: "If you want what I have, then do what I've done." Yet I didn't get a sponsor because I trusted no one. I felt an icy contempt toward those who had it together: *I don't want what you had; I don't want your kids. I don't want your white picket fence. I want to recover, build my own life, and be on my way.* I railed against dogma, expectations, and molds; I felt defiant about how getting sober should look.

Ah, but the women.

After every meeting, they'd embrace me and tell me to keep coming back, tempering my rage. Their acceptance was my first breakthrough. Those hugs were Source's way of reaching me with tentacles: *I'm going to hold on to you with this and this and this and this, and escort you into sobriety with the help of these people.* Little by little, I opened up. Our connection grew deeper as I took in their stories. I kept going back to be surrounded by a supportive community as they loved me for where I was — they loved me until I loved myself.

After establishing a fledgling sense of safety, I dove into AA without a parachute. I didn't realize the importance of community until I encountered the highs and lows of the "pink cloud." This is a term used by those in the program to describe the initial feelings of elation and euphoria in early sobriety. After all the pain and despair I was used to, being part of something greater than myself and living a clean lifestyle created a natural high. So, I floated on my pink cloud, right into my group every week, where people tolerated me. I'm sure some were cringing when I rolled up in the parking lot: *Oh Lord, she's here again!* But others were proud.

I'd long hidden my pain in bottles and pills and food and sex, all the while aching to drop the shield and let others witness me on a soul level. In the rooms, I could again be front and center, just like I had been as a young child in Dad's home and at ABOUT ME FOR ME camp. Only this time, there were no negative consequences for speaking my truth. As often as I could, I marched myself right to the front of the room. Sharing my story as I basked in the attention of my people was baptism-on-demand. I unmasked myself before the group, reveling in the experience of feeling washed anew.

While learning to drop my mask was difficult, accepting that others wanted to see behind it was even harder. I'd worn it so long, as it was the only way I knew how to survive. Behind the mask, I was a twisting conglomeration of ego, pain, despair, and drunkenness. In the room, they wanted every part of the real me, so I pulled down the mask and exposed my face. I discovered that I could be one hundred percent present in my skin and mind, and they received me where I was, as I was. Slowly, their acceptance opened the door for me to stop being fearful of my own demons, and discover myself.

It was in the rooms where I learned how to be in a relationship with others and how to engage issues head on. All of my other relationships didn't want this side of me; they only wanted the party favor, the one who could dance and drink and still be up for awesome sex. Now I could delve into stories of neglect, being raped, dropping out in ninth grade, and being dumped.

And running.

And running.

And running.

Those rooms provided a place to empty my black trash bags

for good.

In AA, we shared our stories, and behind the podium on speaker night, we'd share what it was like, what happened, and what it's like now. We shared our ESH: Experience, Strength, Hope. The podiums in those rooms gave me a place to connect to others, and to connect to Source. So, to use their language, I *surrendered*. You want me, Source? *Well, you got all of me — the good, the bad, the everything. You're going to take it all.*

And Source did.

As my time multiplied in those rooms, I saw the fruit of my labor in exponential ways. I felt good, and others mirrored my process back to me. I would hear, "Oh my God, you're getting better!" I'd be treated to celebratory coffee, and the sweetness of life returned.

One thing I was grateful for was that the program also facilitated strong boundaries among people who needed them. We learned relational skills as we grew together. In certain ways, my distrust worked to my advantage. The human ego of another could not mislead me — not in my life, nor in those rooms. This was new, as someone had always infringed upon my boundaries. I knew to continue on my path; I had to keep a hedge of protection around me. My healing was between Source and I alone; I could not afford to get swept up into the chaos of others. And there was plenty to get swept away in! Healing people are messy. It was the ideal training ground for me to understand who I had control over: only Jewels. It was my responsibility to be her protector, advocate, and friend.

Freed from the numbness of alcohol, the world blossomed around me. I could feel the day. I experienced the wind blowing as Source wrapping arms around me. When I felt that sensation in the middle of the afternoon, it was a reminder I was not alone. Things like that warmed my heart and opened me up to life on an unfamiliar level. These experiences compiled, and my life improved. I walked over glass to get there, but the pain of awareness was well worth the journey.

I got sober and not only me, but everything around me changed.

I was lucky in that mine was not a slow journey — as recovery is for some — and my life quickly catapulted to all new heights. I was already in pain, so I was used to feelings of discomfort. That's how I entered sobriety and stayed there. I embraced my bit of power about who I was and how I wanted to present myself in whatever form. I stepped into control and reclaimed my identity.

Step Four in the process is that we *made a searching and fearless moral inventory of ourselves*. And in my case, I was at my wit's end, utterly exhausted from carrying around on my back all the other people and the things they'd done to me. I'd had enough and was ready to release that anger. I wanted everything out of me that did not belong. Shedding that skin unveiled more and more of me.

Part of the growing process is to look at things within yourself which includes belief systems, experiences, or anything that conflicts with your authentic being. You might think you have to keep this to yourself and figure it out on your own. But you don't. Consider an elephant with a thorn in her foot. When you look at the outside, everything looks fine. But if you think that for the last year that elephant has been walking around on that thorn, she's been growing increasingly more uncomfortable without a solution. This analogy equates to a full year of feeling every step of that thorn, and you can see how it's more courageous to stay in sobriety than it is to return to that numbness.

There are things that pull you as opposed to things that push you. And whatever was in those rooms was pulling me. I wasn't being pushed, and that's what recovery is all about: the willingness to be pulled to something as opposed to being pushed into it. My bar had sunk so low that I'd become invisible in the world. But not anymore.

I straddled two worlds, my professional life in healthcare, and my personal life, where I was getting clean. When I entered the group, they greeted me warmly, and I felt important, like a bona fide member. I had some ownership in knowing that no matter what I did or how I acted — I could not lose my seat in the rooms. The relationships I made in the rooms would not implode. I wouldn't need to throw my shit into yet another black garbage bag and hit the highway. I could not fuck up those relationships, and I took great comfort in that reality. We were almost a family unit, but not the kind that ignores you and crosses boundaries without your consent. For the first time, I felt safe. The women in those rooms would never walk away. The men in those rooms would never leave. It was my group, and I was proud to belong.

When I passed an important milestone and began to work with other people in the rooms, I learned how healing looked different for everyone. I was eager to help others, confident I had that whole Big Book thing down. I assumed my role, albeit it somewhat co-dependent, in picking up and brushing off the next drunk who walked in. That created a lot of purpose for somebody like me, who was eventually asked to leave any other scenario. I took great pride in encouraging our newly sober family members. In fact, this process gave me a sense of how good it felt to serve those who were healing.

Like any other part of life, there were difficulties. People I'd invested time and energy into fell out and started drinking again. In the beginning, I would take it personally and feel angry: *I gave you everything you need! What did you do? Why did you go back out?* I gave a ride to a lady whose boyfriend was in the hospital, and when she disappeared from the waiting room, I found her in the gift shop chugging a bottle of Scope. Ultimately, she died of her disease, which devastated me, and I took it on emotionally. At that stage of my sobriety, I was giving with no boundaries. Which I learned can be an addiction of its own.

It makes sense, after addiction has devoured so much of yourself. It doesn't feel normal to have access to every part of yourself. By default, I'd ration out my energy with the best intentions to help everyone else in the way it had helped me. It took a while to learn that the successes and failures of others were not my own. I eventually learned not to take responsibility for the slip-ups of other group members. As I have grown and evolved, I have realized the larger picture in that our paths and our honor are sacredly our own, and there's no real stepping out of line. We make mistakes, and we can get back on track or not.

If I had been one hundred percent present for the duration of disease, I might not be here today. If I would have been able to receive one hundred percent of my environment, with no escape, I believe it would have broken me. I consider my numbness and blackouts a blessing. My vice tempered my pain just enough to keep me from taking my life. Some of my blackouts were Source's gift to my sanity; I never want to work through or dig up what was happening when I was out of touch. I just want to keep going and acknowledge that I no longer need a vice for protection; I am now internally resolute enough to face the world, forgive the past, and grow from the pain. Though some pains are still insufferable.

Playing with fire had been my ultimate addiction; I'd long sought thrill to temper the pain of my life and distract me from my choices — which, ironically, snuffed out all of my best options. As a byproduct of this pattern, each new relationship was always a little worse than the one before, until finally, I hit emotional and spiritual bankruptcy. And there was nothing left. I was barren, right down to the bone, the marrow of my life sucked dry. My only remaining options were to forfeit or to keep going. And I found in those rooms, despite my circumstances, a glistening strand of hope: the will to live.

With my sober eyes, I recognized Steph was functioning, but she wasn't thriving. This complicated our relationship, because I wasn't sure how to exist around her. She didn't seem like she cared about improving her life for her own wellbeing, and this lack of trajectory created a rift between us. I didn't know how to gauge people who were not in recovery or making a mess of their lives, nor discern if it was okay to have a beer every day after work while in recovery. Some people function that way all their lives. Steph wasn't exactly a mess, but she wasn't growing either. I couldn't discern if she was a hindrance to my work.

I got sober in March and the answers became increasingly apparent. When I went into recovery, I tilled the topsoil of myself, and my authenticity sprouted and came into full bloom. I was wholly Jewels for the first time. Then, at the most minute levels, I felt the differences between Steph and I. And I still hadn't even properly started working the steps. I'd only been integrating into the AA community at that point, so my emotions were still like tiny nerve endings all over me. I didn't know how to process the reality that our relationship was eroding; I didn't want to accept that sometimes two people can have different orientations toward the same goal.

In our case, we both said we wanted to be healthy, but we were not growing in the same direction, nor at a similar pace. My feelings permeated everything, sucking all the oxygen out of the room. There was so much undoing to be done and so much becoming to work through, and I saw that I was in no state to be in a relationship. Steph had Jennifer and Alicia to bounce things off of and use for a source of support through my transition, and I'm sure that was very helpful for her.

As reality pressed down on me, I raged at her and said, "This is not who I am! This is not what I want! I'm going to live in the guest bedroom and I will pay you rent until I find my own place," I could tell I hurt her, but I knew the difference between hurt and harm. Steph didn't have the same relationship to rock bottom as I did. She was okay with her status in life, and her level of drinking seemed to work for her, just not for me. I grieved for the loss, but I had to go. Staying was not an option. I moved out, and this time I used boxes and suitcases.

I continued to work at the hospital and went back to college part time. But sobriety wasn't a smooth ride; let nobody tell you it's going to be. In the rooms, we meet different people. We do things differently than we had before because we get sober. You don't become a different person, and as the saying goes, you can clean up a horse, but there's still always going to be a horse under that dirt. I have countless examples of remaining a horse in my life, but perhaps my worst is that, in my first few months of sobriety, I had an affair with a married guy. It got messy, and he ended up moving away. I created a lot of unnecessary turbulence for myself, and others around me. This is how I was used to functioning. I may not have been drinking, but I had a lot to learn about moral behavior.

Nine months is the miracle marker for many people because they say that's where the shift takes place. You think, *Hey! I can do this!* At nine months, I got my first apartment in my name and although I was 35 years old; it was such a mark of accomplishment for me. I'd gotten close with a man who was so financially comfortable he offered to co-sign on the lease. I smiled and shook my head no. *I have this,* I thought. *For the first time I'm going to do this; I have my own back.*

The apartment was a dive, as it was what I qualified for and right after I moved in, there was a shooting across the way in the other building. I didn't care: it was my first sanctuary. I bought my furnishings from Craigslist, and carefully pieced together what was, to me, a beautiful apartment for me and my two cats. I did anything and everything I could to make that little apartment my home. And I was so proud of it. I even painted a wall a super dark purple just because I could.

One evening, as I was washing the Tupperware dishes (because I owned nothing fancy), I looked up at an old phone jack on the wall and saw two little antennae peeking out. *Oh, no, cockroach, you are not living here!* From where I come from, if you have roaches, you are dirt. I grabbed a roll of masking tape and my cats stared at me as I ripped a few strips off and closed that hole. I guess you could say that everything in my life was a similar analogy, and I patched myself together little by little the best I could.

Slowly, like those antennae, the imposter living in my being peeked out from beneath the layers of habit and energy and circumstance. I felt the shift breaking me open as I battled everything foreign that was within me. I embraced the art of letting go and learned to stop resisting and allowed myself to surface.

As I surrendered, Jewels emerged.

CHAPTER TEN

~/|\~

Play the Tape Out

I n recovery, I learned to do what they called *play the tape out*, a phrase we use when we're in the middle of an uncertain situation. We're told to play the tape out to see what the typical outcome would probably be. I had so much catching up to do. The list seemed endless, and by the time I checked off one box, another one or two or ten would appear at the end. I started with my physical health, and in particular, my dental health.

I felt such shame when going to the dentist, loathing the idea of having my teeth cleaned. My previous lack of dental care rendered any work on my teeth so very uncomfortable. The dental hygienist would scrub and file and pick and shine to get my teeth in semi-tolerable condition. And after her efforts came the dentist for the evaluation! Oh, how I hated to hear the long list of repairs needed, the lack of this and that, and if I didn't do this, I risked losing even more teeth.

As I learned the ropes of my new life, I knew it wouldn't be healthy for me to comply with pre-existing dogma, aside from routine dental care. Dogma hadn't worked for my mother — only yielding toxicity and abuse — and it would not work for me. So, I took the steps to construct a life according to what worked for me and me alone; I had no connections or obligations outside of Source.

See, they expected females of my generation to do what they expected of us. When people from my past reached out to me, they expected me to be gracious and respond, but in recovery I threw off that mantle. And by God, did that feel absolutely delicious. Going off the rails when I was drinking fueled that inner defiance within me that helped me break all the previous molds in sobriety.

Recovery came replete with family in the rooms who encouraged me to break those old patterns instead of facilitating them with shame. My recovery family supported me with grace through the layers and complications of healing. Learning that family does not have to be biological was invaluable and freeing, as I learned how to find the love and connection I'd always deserved.

It was liberating to take in that Robert and his family were Mom's choices — not mine. I learned to separate the two and ditched the obligation to behave how they expected me to. When I had been drinking, I had made a phone call to Bobby while driving home from a therapy appointment. I screamed at him, "Do you know the impact you have made on the rest of my life?" I was so full of hate and aggravated grief before sobriety. What little sense I had back then was eclipsed by my anger, so I felt grateful to be on the side where I could express myself in the rooms without taking the paint off the walls.

If I was going to stay sober, I had to find something that brought me to sanity. So I found sobriety in the sun on my skin; it dried me out and warmed me to the world around me. The breeze taught me how to breathe, and to recognize my part in something greater than myself. It was as if the entire universe came to live inside me; I was a part of the sky and the heavens, and I could bring that heaven right down to earth with me. And have hope. That hope was a divine hug from Source when I tired of pushing everybody away.

The first time as an adult that I saw a picture of Robert was when I found his Facebook account. I probably shouldn't have even looked into it, but I was curious. It amazed me how time can shrink monsters to mere men. Robert was old, nearly unrecognizable. His long, white hair hung down either side of the chest I remembered at eye-level. The many offspring in his public photos stood faded and haunted alongside him. Although I didn't know who they were, I feared for them. Robert stood in the same stance that he always took when beside my mother, the same person, but so much smaller than the place he occupied in my memory. Seeing him adult-to-adult evoked thoughts of, *I'm bigger than you today.* But I was always bigger than him, even as a powerful, innocent soul in a small helpless frame. After all, it took a pretty small man to do what he did.

It pinches to reconcile that both of my parents died in their attempts to get better, while Robert still lives. While I would never wish death upon another, the reality of my abuser's survival paired with my last memory of my father will never not be a source of heartache. I was only ever stolen from; and Robert lives on, continuing to leech energy from the earth. On my better days, I send him healing prayers. But I'm not going for sainthood, just sanity.

While I wonder if he thinks about me or regrets his choices, I don't have a desire to reach out to him or his remaining broken children. I have no desire to show them what I've become. I always thought I would want to do that, and it surprised me to discover that sobriety washed away any desire to seek approval. I no longer wished to tamper with my carefully constructed sanctuary. I might spend the rest of my life trying to forgive Robert.

But not for him — for me.

When you forgive, you energetically cut the cords between that person and yourself in your being. And I've done that in a lot of different circumstances, many times. So when my mind would wander toward the idea of showing folks from my past who I've become, it was easier to just keep walking. I recognized the ego in those thoughts, because I would only expect that I was better than another. Well, that's not my way of living any longer.

Now I have the choice to sit down with somebody like Robert on my own terms, unlike when I was a child. To be in his presence would introduce a level of energetic connection that I did not hold; a level of acceptance I am not sure I'll ever know. Some people think we have an obligation to stand before another and offer our forgiveness. Good manners dictate we must behave in such a way. Women should turn the other cheek. In fact, several healing modalities are centered around this kind of practice. They note it's beneficial to do the necessary work to repair relationships with your abuser. Family is *blood*, and there's some sort of biological need to seek reparation.

I disagree.

Wholeheartedly.

Sometimes it's better to move on, especially if you fantasize about running into these people in a dark alley, which is residual anger talking. Reconciling abuse can take years to overcome, so it's not wise to venture into past relationships, even in the name of healing. I alchemized the pain in my efforts toward growth and do better in the future. I moved forward, choosing to be hyper aware of toxic energy; I exited when I noticed its presence, no matter how compelling the scenario appeared. Often, I recognized that call to old patterns, knowing I couldn't risk it. I worked on metaphysical levels, coming to understand how we can absorb somebody toxic within our circle. It's a direct offense to our physical and energy bodies; even the toxicity coming through the TV screen can shift my whole evening. The more I put boundaries on my energy, the better.

I tried to bring healing into every new situation and circumstance I encountered. I looked for ways to belight, and bring myself into a different, higher vibration. I became mindful of my sense of power and freedom, seeing it as a gift and a responsibility. We learn in recovery that we are supposed to live freely; the beauty of being free means shedding resentments. I learned to bypass resentments before they started with a healthy presence, good boundaries, and exiting early if need be.

And that's not to say I got it right every time, then or now. I have hard days. Rock bottom changed me, catalyzing my climb toward the other side of life, but it did not erase me. I was still there, still living inside the body assigned to Jewels. It's like riding a bicycle. If I did not fall and bleed, I would not learn balance. And I'm not suggesting that everybody has to go through the level of pain I did, but what I encountered made me as strong as I am today. So I learned that to sit and wallow in pain meant I was missing the purpose.

I didn't subscribe to victimhood, as that implied that I was inferior in surrendering my power to someone else. I believe in a divine intelligence higher than my paygrade: it's not good, it's not bad, it just is. When I took that concept and shined that light on the series of events that happened in my life, yes, they were uncomfortable, and yes, they were chaotic — but they gave me different ways of seeing and doing things. I believed that I had to endure all these things to come into wholeness.

I always found some sort of love, whatever that was. I survived because no matter how dark it got, that common thread of Source within kept bringing me through to the light again. I moved over here and I moved over here and I kept moving forward. That was a gift from Source, that gift to thrive and to continue, no matter what. I still try to make it look good, but I thrived and I pushed and I pulled through, and I think that was Source spurring me on. No matter what I faced in my earlier days of recovery, I pursued Source. I pursued sobriety. And I protected myself.

We all have to heal and abide by our own wisdom. We all have to hit ground zero. Recovery gave me that rock bottom opportunity to lay a strong foundation and then build a life upon it. Once I threw off the dogmas, my new, naked life took me in directions I had not anticipated.

CHAPTER ELEVEN

⁓⁓

Displacement by Death

I learned a great deal from Mom as her actions — and inactions — taught me a lot. She was a perfectionist to the fullest, starting every day, weekend or not, with a shower and a face full of makeup. As a child, I remember sitting next to her on the toilet stool as she put her wet brush into her pasty Mary Kay eyeliner to make the most perfect cat's eyes. Mom was very proper and expected me to be the same. From her, I learned impeccable table manners and the importance of beautiful posture.

I appreciate some of her lessons, but neither direction nor discipline was her strong suit. I had long pleaded for Mom to get into counseling. Our parent daughter role switched once I moved out of the house. I took on more of a parental role with her regarding her emotions, because she struggled in that area. We shifted into a friendship dynamic and it suited us.

In April 2007, Mom gave me my 30-day chip — and I wouldn't have chosen anyone else. I was so proud to meet her eyes and take in her smile as that chip passed from her fingers to mine. Around November of that year, she developed an ongoing respiratory issue that she couldn't shake. After a lot of prodding from me, she went in for tests, but we had to wait over Christmas for the results.

In the first part of the new year, she received the diagnosis:

stage four lung cancer. The news took us completely by surprise as she was only 60 years old and seemingly healthy. I didn't know what to do with such a dire prognosis, and I shudder to think of how I would have fared had I still been drinking. But recovery gave me some tools to do the nitty gritty work of being a good human. I prepared to move to her state to be with her where I could work and hold up the household as she had done for me multiple times.

Even though Mom wasn't what you would call emotionally available, she was my rock. She was always there to guide me on the best choice according to her process. When she got sick while I was focusing on getting sober, I started feeling again instead of being completely suppressed. And as my feelings developed into a healthier expression, I could love my mom more and more. It was a special gift to grow into the energy of love for her.

I had met a gentleman in the rooms of recovery who would, around that time, briefly become my husband. He worked as an air traffic controller and offered to fly me back and forth to Florida. I took him up on his offer and this friendship evolved into a sturdy love. Thomas was from a large Southern Baptist family, and feeling embraced by an entire group of people made me eager to join the fold. I married him in a quick wedding, which held the purpose of supporting me while Mom declined, then died nine months later. Thomas's family stepped in at just the perfect time to provide the support I needed.

More than a few miracles took place as Mom transitioned into death. For example, when she had a cancerous lobe removed, during surgery the doctor saw that the disease had spread into her lymph nodes. He felt it was necessary to remove an entire lung. I was in the waiting room by myself during her surgery, and when the doctor came out to tell me the news, I crumpled.

In the rawness of that moment, in the recovery of my new life, the doctor's dire news stunned me. When he returned to take care of my mom, I sat alone trying to make sense of the change in circumstance. In the waiting room was a big circle of women who clearly all knew each other as they were talking as a group. I walked up to them with tears running down my face and said, "I know that I don't know any of you, but my mom has had a lung removed and I need a hug."

Every single woman gave me a hug, just as if I was one of their own. That's the moment I recognized the power of feminine energy and how loving and nurturing it is. They were unfamiliar, yet I felt all the love in their embrace present for me, even as a stranger. We don't choose our angels, and they always seem to find us. Those ladies were my six divine angels sitting outside waiting for me. Just as when I was in the rooms of recovery, it was the hugs that did it for me. Hugs were such a different touch; it was something that mom could never offer when I was younger in the midst of only receiving touches that did significant damage. When you hug, your hearts are next to each other and there's a lot of energetic healing that takes place in that exchange. My meter was at such a low level that any dose of actual love filled me right back up.

I sat in the ICU with Mom after her surgery as she was coming to, still highly medicated. I was learning about the power of energy, specifically through the warmth of the sun and the breeze that would envelop and comfort me. I was experiencing life at a core level; with all my senses wide awake, I was more aware than I'd ever been before. I was present, and this presence gave me the opportunity to heal my mom. I put lotion on my hands and touched the only part of Mom that was not covered in cables and wires and monitors: her feet. I gave my mom a foot rub, all the while thinking, *I'm pouring love into you. I'm pouring love into you. I'm pouring love into you.* That was a profound moment that I got to see and feel in my heart. To be present, to offer that sort of loving contact to her was healing for me. The touch. The love. The giving.

Mom went downhill so fast, snowballing straight to the end. There was the day she said, "I'm not feeling strong. I think I'm going to spend the night at my friend's house on the couch." She could no longer get up and care for herself as her condition progressed. During her subsequent treatment, she called me one day and said, "I'm heading in for a routine blood transfusion."

"Mom, there is no such thing as a routine blood transfusion," I replied, shaking my head at her delusion. Despite the prognosis, she continued to wear the mask. Everything was fine. She was going to do some gardening. She would keep up with her routine. That little transfusion was going to take place in a beautiful hospice. Mom had always been small, but she was so frail by then with scattered slivers of hair on her head. But she still had that personality I knew as my indomitable mom.

Right before death, many people experience a real anxiousness that causes one to move a lot. Death tremors, I think they call it. It's as if you have all this crazy energy that screams, *Hey! Get me out of this body!* When Mom reached that stage, they had to medicate her to soothe the jitters of leaving her body. It was as if she was grieving the life she never fully got to live, nor enjoy; longing for the seasons that her weaker choices had stolen.

During one of my visits, the tech said to me, "I wanted to let you know that on Wednesday, I was helping your mom into the bathroom and I asked her, 'Do you realize that you're going to die?' Your mom said, 'That's what they said.' I asked her, 'Well, what do you think about that?' She's in denial that this is even going down." For better or for worse, survivor mode was my mom's superpower.

Despite what headed our way, I would not leave her side. I was going to make sure it ended beautifully for her; wanting the ending to restore dignity to the beginning. Her decline reached the point where I had to make that call to Justin, but as I dialed repeatedly, I figured out that he wouldn't take my call from my number. When I called from Mom's phone, he answered, and I said, "Justin, I know you don't want to talk to me, but it's about Mom so please don't hang up." I gave him the update, and he said that he and his wife would be there the next day, which gave us a 24-hour window.

I was determined to keep Mom alive until Justin and his wife Rory arrived. I sat by Mom's side as she drifted in and out of consciousness as the drugs took her back and forth like the tide. She couldn't conduct full sentence conversations anymore, offering only bits and pieces of words and sounds. I crawled into bed with her, both of us wearing our pajamas, just as I had liked to do when I was a little girl.

People with lung cancer tend to curl forward as perhaps opening the back makes more space to breathe. My mom had adopted this posture and had incorporated a rocking motion. So when I got into the bed with her, I wrapped my arms around her, rocking as I talked and cried and talked and cried. I kept telling her that Justin and Rory were on their way. I kept it constant so she would hang on and stay alive.

It was about two o'clock in the afternoon the next day when Justin and Rory walked in. Mom said, "Justin, Justin, Justin, Justin, Justin, Justin, Justin, Justin." That's all she could say. It was beautiful as the three of us were in the same room together, something she'd tried to orchestrate for the past seven years. Justin started to cry, and I got out of the bed so they could share time together.

Too soon we reached the point where the nurse said, "Why are you still here? You have to leave." I didn't understand. I wanted to stay until the end. To witness her transition from life, just as she had witnessed my entrance. The nurse explained, "She won't die if you're here."

That made sense. I'd been saying to her, "Mom, go. You don't have to stay anymore. Be at peace. Mom, I'm telling you, you can go. We're all here. Everything is fine. Now you can go." We'd said our goodbyes and made our amends. Days passed. But she just wouldn't go. For as rough as life can be, you'd be surprised how hard a person can fight to stay alongside their loved ones. I considered her gumption as the strength she wished she'd had when we were kids. She was staying for us, with a power she didn't possess in either of her marriages. Though we forgave her, she needed to show up for her children to recompense; so she endured.

At the nurse's suggestion, we left that night after saying what we already knew would be our final goodbyes. The next morning we got the call informing us that she had died. I was a year sober in March 2008 and my mom died on September 11, 2009.

Then I was at a round table with my brother and his wife, signing papers for Mom's cremation. We went to her trailer and witnessed that she had been in complete denial that her time on earth was drawing to a close. While cleaning out her home, we saw that it looked as if she expected to return at any time. We had to take the dishes out of the dishwasher and fold a load or two of laundry.

You can know a person and not know them at the same time. And so it was that alone in her space — without her — Justin and I learned about all of her little behaviors. Because I no longer lived with her, it gave me separation from her and her peculiarities. She had what she called the kid's wall, which was chock full of all our pictures from over the years. From the years that included Robert and his family, she had taken scissors to their faces and bodies, cropping them out. If only it were that easy.

Like me, Mom didn't trust anybody. She was a very secretive woman and Justin and I soon burned through two different electric shredders going through all her files. We learned that when she was told of her diagnosis; she took out the money from her 401k, which was a hefty $65,000 that she had tucked away. According to her documentation, she gave her brother all that money to hold. We learned through her ledgers that every time he visited; he ferried the amount of money that she requested, acting as her bank. Mom kept a record of every transaction and exactly how much money he was holding.

When Justin contacted him to ask about the money, our uncle said, "I don't know what you're talking about. Your mother didn't give me any money."

He kept it all. Every single penny. Once again, and at the end of her life, Mom had trusted an untrustworthy person.

Justin's portion of the inheritance would have helped him hang on to their home that was going into foreclosure. But our uncle refused to admit that he had Mom's money, despite our pleading with him. So Justin took most of Mom's belongings and packed them into her car and drove it home. They drove the car until the registration ran out. And when the trailer Mom had bought from her brother went into foreclosure, her brother went to the bank and bought it back at a foreclosure price, making money from her at our expense even in death.

Mom's absence left a gaping hole that signaled a momentous shift in me. I did not seek to fill that void — with anything. I sat with it. Although I could grieve on my own, I longed to shoulder a shared grief with family. Thomas's family didn't know me long enough to understand my loss. They gave me a couple of weeks to grieve, but they'd never met my mom. My loss was not that of my husband's family, and I felt very alone.

I felt displaced after Mom's death because I didn't have that constant love, which I realized had been an extremely beneficial thing for me to have. I believe that her love — albeit imperfect — was what kept me alive for the first 34 years of my life. Even at her worst, Mom grounded me. And once she left, Source could come in and peel the layers of the onion back, allowing my emotions to seep out.

I believe that if Mom would've lived through the duration of my full recovery, she would have inhibited my growth. I would have continued to look to her for guidance when I needed to learn how to govern myself. Her advice wouldn't have benefited me any more than it had when I was young. It was no coincidence that Mom died so close to the one-year anniversary of my sobriety. The first year in recovery is when you get physically sober. The second year you get emotionally sober. And in the third year, you explore spiritual sobriety. When Mom passed, I was on the road to addressing my emotional sobriety.

Mom's passing was not devastating for me, though I worried at first that I would lose every ounce of my being when she died. But recovery gave me the tools to understand that her death was more about learning what comes next, about how things could be. Sometimes, in my recovery success, I mourned how I would have loved for Mom to reap the benefits of the materialistic rewards of my life. Or that she could have been there to experience that Thanksgiving I celebrated later that year with my brother. But perhaps if that alternative life had taken place, none of the rest would have passed.

As I continued to evolve, grow, and become clear on who I was in my physical body, and to discover my identity in society, I better understood Mom's position. For example, when I witnessed the female struggle with work/life balance, I experienced the internal doubts that women have in supporting themselves. Sober, I could see the entire picture, and feel the magnitude of how it's difficult to be a woman in the world. I adopted grace for my mother, whose life had not been easy. She was born into striving and lived her entire life that way, always treading water, even in the best of times. I slowly developed a bigger appreciation for Mom and life itself in the time after her passing.

When you do Step Four or Step Five in recovery, you identify all your resentments. Naturally, my feelings for Mom came up when I reached these milestones. As I entered deeper stages of vulnerability, I brought my past through the steps and began forgiving. There are bits that I have yet to process. But I've learned that grief takes time, possibly the rest of my life, and that's okay.

In order for me to reconcile what happened, I have to access empathy. I have to see my oppressor as another soul, another child of God. I can forgive the situation, but for me to forgive that person, I have to open myself beyond my defenses. My adoption of this momentous process helped me expand beyond my earlier hurts.

And later that year, when my brother Justin invited me to his home to spend Christmas with his family, it catalyzed the mending of our relationship. The knitting process of the reunion was fraught with discomfort for me, and for Justin's family. I felt like the proverbial family member returning from prison and trying to catch up with all the new technology. Everybody had grown up while I was living in another life as I tried to make amends for yesteryear. By the time Christmas arrived, they'd done their grieving for Mom as a family, and when I wanted to share my grief, they shook their heads and changed the subject.

I quickly discovered that once in sobriety, I didn't know the rules for being a sister. When Justin threw a house-warming party, I didn't know what to do or not do. I stood awkwardly off to the side, mute; half-worried I would embarrass them. I recognized that the reason so many things had been disastrous for me was because I didn't understand traditional roles. I took things at face value and learned that not everyone did. For example, I knew how to arrive at a bridal shower, but I didn't know how to take part, or what the expectations would be; I didn't know what the value and tradition of a baby shower entailed. I hardly even had appropriate clothes to wear, and I knew I stuck out. Without the band-aid of drugs and alcohol, I had a lot of catching up to do; it was as if I was entering the world for the first time.

I walked onto a new planet — Planet Reality — where everything was foreign and no one knew me. I had no history in that realm. Though I was fully present and awake, I didn't know the rules for sober living. I had to learn the *supposed to* while trying to avoid yet another *shouldn't have*. Defiant by nature, I wanted to learn social norms, where perhaps I'd swung too far the other way prior to recovery, without bending to established norms. This meant learning to adult around other adults, which was a blessing and an opportunity to design my original template for what it means to be a woman.

CHAPTER TWELVE

⌐⁄ı⌐

Losing One Man and Finding Another

Immediately after Mom's passing, I returned to my marriage to Thomas. It seemed like the most practical choice. I was in a cerebral place; it was challenging to process her death without a sounding board, so I assumed having a partner would be better than going at it alone. I attended my meetings, but it was never enough. I was grieving inside. I had met Thomas in the rooms, so I imagined he would understand me better than someone who had never been in recovery.

I worked on developing a closer relationship with my dad, and after Thomas and I got married, along with his son, we went to stay with Dad and his partner, Tonya, for a full 5 days. It was a lot for me to process, but I was at the stage of *fake it 'til you make it*. I wanted to show Dad I was a normal daughter now: married, sober, and able to parent stepchildren.

My new adventure with Thomas infused my life with meaning. I believed I could finally experience sobriety to the fullest, with someone alongside me who shared my values and understood the trenches of recovery. Our marriage meant I had to open up to the idea of being a stepmom and a mentor. My mom had been a stepmom, but not a great one, and in some ways I relished the opportunity to do it better. It felt good to sink into something safe. But it wouldn't be long before I learned that committing to an addict comes at a cost and that our new life might be too good to be true.

In the rooms, when we would attend meetings, I would see Thomas thriving in his life beyond drinking. But later I was spurred to notice that he was being deceptive; not everything was as it seemed. Thomas worked as an air traffic controller, and I knew he had already had citations and was on probation because of his drug addiction. Years before, he'd suffered an ankle injury. If he went to any hospital anywhere in the United States and they took an X-ray, he told me they were definitely going to give him codeine. All he had to do was ask.

Thomas had three kids, two girls and one boy. While he drove his children home after a weekend visit, I noticed that Thomas was growing increasingly unresponsive. He suddenly went into a seizure while making a left turn. From the passenger seat, I grabbed the wheel and turned the car while his daughter screamed from the back seat, "He's using again!"

I cried, "What do you mean? No, he's not. He's sober!" I pulled the car to the side of the road.

She said, "No, he's not! I'm done. I want no more of this!" She got out of the car and slammed the door while I was trying to take care of Thomas. I called his sister, who was the reigning queen of the family, then called the ER where I worked to say that my husband seized and we would come through triage. I went straight into nurse mode. But when Thomas recovered, he said that he didn't want to go to the hospital. He mumbled that he wanted to go home. That was my sign. I felt the familiar sinking feeling of knowing the truth, then heard the voice of toxic, empathetic hope rise and say, "Well, maybe not."

Back at home, Thomas rested on the couch while I took a shower. When I came out, I heard him talking to his ex-wife on the phone. And when I heard him confess, "I did it again," I felt that familiar sinking feeling in my stomach, feeling betrayed in every capacity. During our marriage, I didn't know he was using, yet he called his ex-wife to confess. She was screaming and yelling so loud I could hear it from where I stood in the hallway. She seemed to be deeply familiar with the truth I ached to bypass. Their conversation suddenly exposed our marriage for the sham that it was.

My inner codependent lifted her head, and I found myself out in my car in the middle of the night because I couldn't sleep. My thoughts raced as I piecemealed all the details and comments of our lives together. In retrospect, I realized Thomas was a sloppy pill taker and that evidence of his using was there the entire time. I thought each pill I found was a one-off, and not indicative of a pattern. I went into overdrive while Thomas seemed to become even more careless and I found pills here, there, and everywhere. Still, I did my best to stick it out while I plotted my next moves.

We enjoyed camping, and during one drive to a site, I spotted a pharmacy bag in the back seat. "Thomas, what's in the bag?" I asked.

He shrugged. "Oh, that's nothing."

My mind raced with stories I wanted to believe as my internal advocate jumped to his defense. "Well, that's a pretty big nothing," I said, trying to eclipse the moment with an open heart, and a desperation to move past it. I chose the truth I needed to hear.

When we stopped at a gas station, Thomas grabbed the bag and tossed it into a big dumpster, determined to prove a point. He got back in the car. "See? It's nothing."

I said, "Either you go get that nothing, and let me sift through it, or you drop me off at home. I am not playing this game. I am not relapsing because of you." My recovery meant so much to me. But he wouldn't do it. I knew. I knew. I deeply knew.

His pill habit quickly became the elephant in the living room. So I did the brave thing, like always. I started going to Al-Anon, realizing I had to tend to myself and take those first steps that I knew had to be taken. I wasn't going down with the rats on the ship the way my mother always had. I'd worked too hard to climb out of those currents. The Al-Anon meetings, combined with my

AA meetings, kept me sane.

Finally, there was the afternoon when Thomas was taking a nap. He'd emptied his pockets on the kitchen counter beforehand, and there I found one pill. And then another. And another — after he'd recently claimed that he was sober. I took a deep breath and listened to the silent room around me. It was the familiar sound of another sad ending. I knew we were done; I would not go through that with him. I recognized he had a disease, and that I was complete with the cycle. It did not crush me to find those pills; it was almost an expectation, and once he fulfilled it, I stepped into the numb resoluteness that would carry me forward into the unknown.

I shook him awake, handed him his pill, and said, "You better take this now, because I'm going to file for divorce." That was it. I moved into another bedroom and continued in my grieving process for Mom without being distracted by Thomas and his children. Our impending divorce allowed me the separation from his family as I could close the bedroom door and grieve as necessary. My obligations were at an end, and I stepped into who I was, ready to go after what I wanted.

Leaving Thomas was the first relationship I ended because I refused to tolerate somebody else's disease. And, for the first time in my life, something within me reared up to protect both me and my sobriety. Endurance and consistency is a lot for anybody, let alone somebody like me who was really uncomfortable taking the highs and lows in life. I was not prideful, but I cherished my sobriety. I earned something that everybody else was proud of too. There was no way that anything — a man or a marriage — was going to put me down.

After Mom passed and I left Thomas, I reclaimed my power as I stepped onto another fresh path. I didn't know what tomorrow would bring, but I knew I was checking other people's diseases at the door. All of Mom's old behaviors stayed behind as I started the next chapter of life in recovery. I didn't need a man. I didn't need to be a stepmom. I didn't want or have to pick up other people's messes. That wasn't what I was on this planet for.

I'd been burned by fire and shaped into a stronger me. From the ashes emerged a refined Jewels, who was reclaiming her power and control.

As I lost Thomas, I gained an even closer relationship with my father.

It always elated him to hear from me, and his excitement was, at times, overwhelming. He urged me to move back to the town where we used to live, unable to understand that it was no longer my home. Yet I did my best to call him every Sunday at 9:00 a.m. Sometimes I could not receive his love, and would snooze the reminder on my calendar for the following week.

I flew to see him at least once a year to spend a long weekend. But I always stayed at a hotel; I couldn't stay at his home overnight. Not that anything bad happened there, but I was uncomfortable being assailed by the constant memory that he was my dad when I was a little girl.

It's true that sometimes you just can't go back home.

I enjoyed hearing about Dad's life, recognizing that he lived a life that did not resemble mine. He kept himself busy eking out an existence, just as I remembered. He farmed chickens, sold eggs by the roadside, tapped maple trees, and sold organic maple syrup. Dad even had a semi-truck load of wood come every year and he and the guys would spend a couple days cutting it and binding it and then selling that as well.

CHAPTER THIRTEEN

─⁻⁄₁∖⁻

Will the Real Jewels Please Stand Up

As I moved away from judgment, inflexibilities, and old hurts, my journey took me to places I could never have imagined. I learned to step lightly so I could embrace the new, sober, Jewels. I surrendered to the tide of myself; and allowed myself to be carried down the wily streams of life by Source. I was no longer afraid of where I was going; for the first time, I trusted.

I rented a room from Rebecca, another single, sober woman with a beautiful home in a nice part of town. Our situation worked out wonderfully as I weathered the tornado of divorce. Thomas and I finalized the paperwork after one of our meetings. It ended where it had begun; and I had to admit it was a sad symbolism to leave him to his own devices, and erratic healing. But it was the first ending I could be proud of, because it was for me. Our ending was not messy, we maintained a good relationship afterward, handling our fate with integrity. I credit recovery for giving me the tools to exit with grace instead of black garbage bags.

This ending ushered in a new beginning: the mental sobriety stage of my second year in recovery where I searched for my true self buried beneath all the layers. It was akin to stripping years of rushed, sloppy paint jobs from the walls of an old house until I was a naked canvas, denuded of all prior beliefs and programming. It was a time to consider my core beliefs and re-write the tapes — with the most malignant being that I had to be married to a man in order to survive. Throughout the process, my strength and faith in myself grew as I found my inner voice.

At the end of AA meetings, the group would join hands to say the serenity prayer. One gentleman in the room reminded me of Robert, and this stranger repulsed me through no fault of his own. While trying to work the spiritual program, and deprogramming the dogma, I just couldn't stomach this man. When he joined the circle, he reached for my hand, and it immediately triggered me. His fat, rough palms sliding into mine reminded me of Robert. Afterward, I told the gentleman that it was nothing personal, but his physical appearance reminded me of one of my abusers. I said I needed him to keep his distance from me until I healed.

He honored my request, and I think he was proud that he could receive such a message and not take it personally — one of the many wonderful things about being in recovery. Our exchange went over well because I came from a place of love. I could step up to defend my sanity. I could have those uncomfortable conversations with people, including the ones that teetered into inappropriateness. I was becoming better at articulating my boundaries, so if I experienced any sort of offensive or sexual innuendo that I did not invite, I would shut it down from a loving space.

As I got my feet beneath me, I dedicated most of my time to establishing my professional life. To help him out, I took on a portion of my dad's maple syrup business and worked on expanding our distribution into the farmer's markets around my area. Keep in mind that I didn't yet know the first thing about business unless I paid for a service and handed over money. So I asked a lot of questions of anyone and everyone, including the people in the rooms. I was feeling empowered with all my new information and freedom from the confines of the old tapes.

It was in recovery that I first saw a man cry, and it was a profound life-changing moment for me to see a male show vulnerability. The toxic masculinity of the men I had known up to that moment melted from my psyche. The moment elicited a sense of purpose deep inside my soul, a fledgling desire to assist men in expressing their buried feelings and identities.

In the way most journeys begin, initially I stepped into the world of BDSM just to explore. While BDSM incorporates certain aspects of sex, including bondage and discipline, domination and submission, sadism and masochism, I easily discovered that only one avenue interested me. As I took those first faltering steps toward realizing my calling, my female dominant side reared her head. I had awoken.

My emerging desire to become a FemDom surprised even me. Like many dreams, it had evolved slowly over the years and chose me. I was initially careful with expressing my interest, as I knew it would certainly take others off guard, but over time I determined it was worth the risk. And when I was told by one potential sponsor that they wouldn't sponsor me because my interests were sinful, I listened to understand their point of view. They believed I was turning my back on God. Although their reaction elicited a fleeting sense of shame within me, I recognized a place in my healing where I knew I had to honor myself. No sense of rejection was too long standing; I could handle anything.

I wondered where I'd even come to be interested in a world I knew so little about. I'd never read about a FemDom, yet the idea felt innate, inspired even, as if I had carried it with me into this lifetime. In the same way I valued all of my other deeply misunderstood attributes, I knew better than to question my divine gifts and talents. I took it as a learning opportunity to identify who I was, and hold fast to her, even if she was interested in something the rest of society wasn't too keen on.

A FemDom is a dominant position that involves the practice of discipline. As a FemDom, the dominant female takes charge of the submissive partner in "scenes" or relationships. The dominance in the exchange between these two consenting adults is psychological; there is no sex involved. A FemDom can dominate through humiliation or mental directives, such as giving direction to the submissive. Domination can also be physical when it involves restraints or items used to elicit pain such as whips or clamps.

As I had already experimented in my previous relationship with Murphy as a submissive, the idea of domination was not new to me. I learned that the power exchange provided the love and connection I sought. Being a submissive brought the attention I also desired, but it was like Cinderella's shoe on the foot of her stepsisters: not quite the right fit.

Through my connections, I was fortunate to meet a Female Domina, Ms. Rita, who was also sober. It was an answered prayer to find somebody like her who was strong in the space where I was heading. Following Ms. Rita, I stepped on a clear path to explore just who I was inside.

As a child, I'd learned to construct many barriers within myself so nobody could permeate the real me and my true essence. As I went through recovery and stripped myself down to my raw, authentic self, I could confidently go into the FemDom world with my newfound spiritual knowledge. I could function out of love and service to others and know my place was not self-driven. As a power greater than myself took care of me, I had no interest in misusing men for my benefit.

As an eager neophyte, I embraced Ms. Rita's mentorship, acquiring a lot of knowledge and wealth in understanding the male psyche. She had a variety of men-in service to her in her household, including a pool man and housecleaner. These men paid her for the honor of offering their service, and in return, she provided a space for them to express the inner desires they couldn't do at home with their wives. These consensual exchanges fascinated me.

For instance, the pool boy was neither a boy nor the handsome *Sancho in a G-string* we usually imagine. This gentleman cleaned her pool in the buff with his cock and balls locked in an electrified chastity cage. Ms. Rita held the electric remote, leaning back in her chair on the patio to smoke her cigarettes while randomly zapping his cage. Water and electricity should scare the ever-living shit out of most people. But not him; he wanted to dance on that edge of risk. I don't know if it was my tomboy side or the desire to be in control, but I absolutely loved it. There was no abuse, just two people having fun in consensual ways.

From Ms. Rita, I learned technique. She introduced me to influencers and educators within the community and I learned how to do what I did, but I already had that understanding of the instruments to provide love and connection because I experienced it myself. I understood it on a soul level.

The more I explored and witnessed, the further I ventured into the unfamiliar area of my heart, mind, and soul. With each whack of a paddle or click of a remote by Ms. Rita, I took yet another couple of steps toward understanding who I was. Gone were the days of stepping out of my body, going into my head to hide, and floating above and away.

There are two ways to experience childhood abuse. First is from the outside as somebody who sees it. Then there is the person who's in the abuse and how they see it. As I progressed into the FemDom world, naturally there were those who stood on the sidelines and pronounced, *Well, she was abused as a child, which means she has to abuse men to take back her power.*

That was neither true then, nor is it true now.

Source must have made me this way because I certainly didn't grow up wanting to enjoy bringing men to their knees. I never imagined myself a Goddess until men treated me like one. As I had been inside the abuse, I knew what it did to a person. I was familiar with that feeling of not being accepted. Of feeling dirty and wrong. I knew what it felt like to hide things about myself in order to survive, as experience taught me that during this abuse I needed to hide and feel small and invisible. The abuse I experienced as a young person didn't cause me to abuse others. Instead, it allowed me to feel empathy for those who felt shut down inside.

As a child at home with my first family, I sat at the head of the table with a voice. Throughout my years in Robert's home until sobriety, the actions of others silenced me. So when I stepped out of the shadows, I came out with a loving vengeance. As I entered the healing aspects of this power dynamic as an adult, I was no longer disempowered. My prior experiences in life transformed those feelings into a superpower as everything that was once considered negative within me transformed into a positive. I was now in the adult world with a knowledge of what it felt like to suppress my needs, desires, and longings. My empathy invited me to see others at their core. And when some other soul, typically a male, would come to me and say, *I can't do this sort of thing in front of my wife, but I really love the physical sensation of being bound and dominated,* I could embrace his vulnerability and make that happen for him.

Ms. Rita was an older, sober FemDom, and she aptly modeled how to be a FemDom while free of drugs and alcohol. Before, I could not engage the world while sober; more times than not, I was lit when going through the motions. But when I removed the numbing effect of drugs and alcohol, I knew I had to be super conscious of My stepping out process. The dominant/submissive relationships are all about exchanges between the two; I had to use My feminine energy to guide men into their submissive realm. It's an energetic power exchange.

I was very much aware that I had to be mindful of who I played with, and who I allowed to be around Me. And as a FemDom in a male-dominant industry, there were men who questioned My power within My domain. Comments like, "You just need a good spanking," were rampant. Even though those kinds of words came from the less mature male Doms, there were quite a few of them around. The first time they advised Me to get a good spanking, it appalled Me. As I came to understand my position as a FemDom, their words merely struck Me as comical.

Under Ms. Rita, I realized the value of what I had and the space I could hold for others while apprenticing. While she was a professional FemDom, I experimented *pro bono* until I realized the love and respect I witnessed. I started by inviting the idea of being brought small gifts. When the boys gave Me yummy-scented candles and gorgeous bracelets, I realized I wasn't much of a savvy businesswoman — yet — but I began to understand what it meant to make an income as a FemDom.

After I worked with Ms. Rita a couple of times, I became comfortable entering the professional realm with people. Soon I started working out of a Dallas dungeon. Since I always had the mindset of a higher society, I marched straight to the top. When most women start out, they feel they have to charge a gradient of $200 or $300 per hour and make their way up.

Well, not Me.

I started at $600 an hour without a second thought. I did not base My charges on an ego trip, as I didn't think I was better than anybody else. Instead, I saw it more like comparing Cartier to Walmart. Never do you walk into Cartier and see a sale on scarves. They never have sales; they don't need to have sales. There is never a buy-one-get-one-free deal going on, because unlike Walmart, Cartier does not discount their products. And that's how I felt about Myself.

Soon, I had a gentleman in service to Me, paul, and together W/we attended lifestyle events in the community. Front and center at the events, I witnessed how W/we each have entities within that must be expressed, even within the conservative area where W/we lived. If it exists, then this type of expression has to come out, and that's why these underground communities grow. Inside, you'll find executives. Business owners. Lawyers. CPAs. CEOs. The men who wanted My services tired of being in charge; they wanted to submit to a powerful woman.

I met a gentleman named david, who was under protection by another Lady. He and I had communicated online and then after meeting, She relinquished Her authority and I placed him under consideration with Me. This then led to his training collar. A level of commitment I would later dissolve due to his dishonesty.

CHAPTER FOURTEEN

~⊰⊱~

Being Scene

S omething that is commonly misunderstood about the FemDom is that She is cruel, rude, and ruthless. Well — maybe, sometimes She is. But She's not a bad or dark soul, but instead, a woman who understands the dynamics between a man and a woman. We expect men to be the provider, the protector, and the one who makes things happen. As a woman, I'm expected to be the nurturer, the loving superior, the disciplinarian. Within the D/s dynamic, these characteristics shift into a more basic expression. The man wants nothing more than for the woman to be happy. And he will go to any length to make it so.

During the summer that david was in service to Me, it enthralled My roommate, Rebecca. She loved witnessing the powerful dynamic of loyalty and servitude, and she quickly became accustomed to O/our Sunday afternoon lunches where david would cook and serve U/us like queens. But eventually she became uncomfortable with My emerging authority and questioned My integrity.

As her Christian background influenced her, Rebecca began to see My relationships with men as harmful. In fact, she labeled them as abusive and asked Me to move out immediately. With little or no resistance, I graciously packed My belongings. I knew

I had bigger things ahead of Me, and I certainly didn't want to be around anyone who didn't support My newfound empowerment.

Despite Ms. Rita's advice that I live on My own, I felt financially insecure and wasn't confident that I could afford to do so. So paul and I rented a functional two-bedroom apartment with a lovely little balcony. It was nothing special, but it was cute, and it was O/ours.

At the time, david was a (very) closeted drinker. In fact, one afternoon after reviewing a receipt of products I'd asked him to buy, I found something that was quite foreign to Me: 6-pack $5.79. I looked at him. "What the hell is this?"

He stood before Me, silent.

I asked again, "david, what is this charge?"

With his head bowed, he answered very softly, "That was for a six-pack of beer, Ma'am."

"Beer! Are you kidding Me! And did you drink all six of these while driving from the store to here?"

"No, Ma'am. Just two. The rest are in my trunk." We walked out to his car, he popped the trunk and there was the cooler with four cans of beer on ice. "Ma'am, I'm sorry. I won't ever do it again," he said.

I looked at him, straight-faced with no expression. "I know you won't. Because you will never be in My presence again. Get your things. You're leaving now."

Once I dismissed david, I appointed paul as My alpha boy; a role where I would expect him to protect Me as My primary servant. With his help, I built My empire. Through the community I learned protocol and the responsibilities of being Head of Household. I acquired two other boys, one who cleaned My home and the other who served Me during lifestyle events and parties. Together, the four of U/us had a blast. And with every passing day, the shoes of Ms. Jewels became a better fit.

There are many customs of the D/s lifestyle that stem from the Leatherman Culture, an early gay male leather subculture. Some loosely practiced the lifestyle as a fantasy, while others practiced as a way of life. There were contracts and collars, discipline, and rewards. There was extensive training and protocols that had to be observed. As Head of Household, I had a lot of responsibilities; primarily that I was liable for My boys' safety, both physically and mentally.

As Ms. Jewels evolved within the community, She also progressed professionally. The persona of an ironclad disciplinarian came to life. As Ms. Jewels, I wore vintage Chanel dress suits, Cuban stockings, and pointed-toe heels. The images on My website would quickly mesmerize My viewer and immediately affirm who was in charge. My choice of words and the tone of My temperament would entice any man with a submissive inclination to seek Me out.

From the moment they visited My website and read My words, the subservient side of the men would stir. Little did they realize; I was setting the stage for their fantasy to become a reality. I listed clear-cut directions on My website for them to follow if they wanted the chance to see Me.

First, I would require them to read My website in its entirety. They had to complete an application that revealed their interests and reasons for wanting to be in My presence. After reviewing their application, I would decide if I felt W/we'd be a good match. Now because there wasn't a reliable resource to screen potential clients, My intuition and experience with men was My guiding authority. From My prior experiences, I could quickly detect any malicious intentions or harmful motives. Some applicants, even after reading My website, would request fetishes I was not interested in carrying out. Scenes such as human burial and kidnapping weren't My thing. I'd simply tell them W/we weren't a suitable match and wish them well on their search.

Being an authoritarian, I truly enjoyed OTK (over the knee) spanking and Domestic Discipline. CBT (cock and ball torture) and sissification were a couple of other areas that I fancied. Now please don't let the word torture set too deep in your mind. I see it more as a shock factor than a form of torment. But that's from the view of the One without the balls.

Sissification is a form of kink where the submissive man takes on a feminine role. Likely, this interest stems from the societal pressure of men to be masculine. These clients greatly enjoyed the ability to role play as women in various ways, including cross-dressing, housecleaning, and applying makeup.

Some men enjoy the pain and discomfort of the hand of a strong, beautiful woman. And I had many practices and instruments to choose from to satisfy their requests: squeezing, pinching, binding, and caging, just to name a few. But let's not get too far from the real reason these delightful men came begging to serve Me. It was the psychological aspect that brought them to their knees.

My ideal client was a high-level executive, CEO, or CFO who would fly in just to see Me. W/we both understood they had other responsibilities and that O/our time together was brief, but everlasting. I typically didn't see single men; I preferred My clients have obligations such as a marriage and children to tend to. That meant they couldn't get too caught up in Me and show up at My doorstep unannounced with their suitcase in hand.

One of the unfortunate aspects of society is that most women have learned to look after others before themselves. The needs of children, husbands, and even peers often come before our own. Somewhere in the process of discovery, if their husbands were to come into the bedroom with a request of bondage, many women have been conditioned to see his request as perverted or sinful.

So instead of taking the chance of being denied or rejected by their loving wives, men would come see Me instead. In My world, I would never see them as demonic or disgraceful. By seeing Me they would never chance losing their marriage, career, or custody of their children. These men saw Me as a safe space to explore and satisfy their burning need for submission.

I did not have sex with My clients, and that was a cement boundary; sex was not on My menu at any price. In Europe, it's customary to have a dominatrix who induces pain and that sort of euphoria. Then there are people who operate in the red-light district and in the black-light district. Sex and D/s are two discrete entities. In the states, we throw everything in together and some mistresses have sex with their clients. But that did not interest Me. I preferred the European style of separation.

As a professional, I walked a fine line of meeting the needs of My clients and staying within the boundaries of the law. The last thing I was willing to do was lose My business and go to jail. I refused to take that risk, which meant that I had to clearly understand how I could operate within the confines of the law. For example, in the state I was in, I could not penetrate a man. That would be seen as prostitution. But I could allow him to penetrate himself and be in accordance with the law. He also could not hand Me the tribute. That would be seen as the practice of engaging in indiscriminate sexual activity in exchange for immediate payment of money or other valuables. So I'd simply request he put his gift of tribute (money) in an envelope and leave it on My counter when he arrived.

After receiving his application, I would wait 24–48 hours to respond. Of course, I was busy and not easily accessible like the other women in his life. I'd follow up with an email requesting a phone date. I would write something along the lines of, *I appreciate your interests in serving Me. I'd like to learn more about you and the possibility of you spending time with Me. I will call you on Tuesday at two o'clock. Will you be available to take My call?*

Keep in mind, I wasn't asking if they had time for Me. Instead, I was asking if they'd be available for Me. I'd also ask that they be in an area where they could speak freely. I never wanted to be inconvenienced by the unexpected walk-in of a colleague. If they'd write back with anything but a "Yes, of course, Ma'am" I'd see it as an inability to satisfy Me and knew that ultimately we wouldn't be a suitable match.

If I agreed to speak with them, I could practically feel their energy reaching My way: *Oh my God, She wants to talk to me!*

During O/our phone conversation I'd continue to feel them out. Did they do as I'd asked? Did they place themself in a position not to be interrupted by anyone during O/our call? Did they pull over so as not to be distracted by traffic during O/our conversation? I had no intention of curbing My requests or changing My tone during My interview process. I asked fairly intimate questions and I paid attention to how they maneuvered themselves in order to answer My questions openly and honestly.

If the call went in their favor, I would invite them to come see Me. I would explain the logistics, My expectations, and remind them of My suggested tribute. With first-time clients I required a maximum of two hours. Sometimes during the excitement of it all, they would ask for four or six hours with Me. With all due respect, I was flattered and would have enjoyed playing with them for that length of time. But for O/our first time, I inevitably erred on the side of caution and limited O/our meeting to two hours.

My clients always knew to bring a little something extra. Either cushioning the envelope or presenting a beautiful gift. Surprisingly, it wouldn't be a candle or long-stemmed red roses but gracious gifts, like fine jewelry or a gift card to a luxury retail store. Those who could spend time with Me often would know that these lovely gifts would set them apart from any others who would be vying for My attention: the beauty of the competitive male.

There was never any written agreement of confidentiality. It was a given. It was expected that when you engage with a woman of My caliber that a solid reputation was also part of the package. There'd be less guaranteed discretion with a lady who'd advertised on Craigslist or City Pages with the rate of $150–$200 an hour for her time. I had credibility and required references from another in order to see Me, something that very few others required.

Within a week of O/our phone conversation, I would schedule O/our time together. Just like any other therapeutic line of work, I kept notes on O/ur interactions and details of O/ur meetings. Since I couldn't take any pictures, I only had names to go by. And since there may be a dozen Jeffs coming through My door, I needed to keep them straight. I certainly didn't want to plan a scene for bondage Jeff when sissy Jeff arrived. These organizational skills were very important to Me and I never made a logistical error, not once.

By the time the day for their visit arrived, My clients would be about to burst at the seams. Men love visuals and My website had many of them to fantasize about during the interim before O/our meeting. One of the many fun things I would request of My clients was that they refrain from orgasm until they see Me, which was typically a four-day window. Much more than that, and they'd start climbing the walls. And I certainly wouldn't want to alarm the wife he had waiting at home. Chastity does interesting things to a man who enjoys control. They become extremely attentive and observant, something that many wives unknowingly enjoyed when her husband was in service to Me.

Many ask if I ever felt threatened or unsafe during a session. And the answer is no. I never felt as if My guest had any ill intentions toward Me. Perhaps it was because of the tone I set and the rigorous interview process I followed. As a part of My recovery program I was and still am in constant contact with My Higher Power, and as a result, I am kept safe. I don't live within the dark energies any longer. I no longer attract those dark energies, either. I asked for Source to keep Me safe during My day, avoiding any harms or indifferences. And just like in the spiritual principles of Step 3, I lived My life by the principles of honesty, open-mindedness, willingness, trust, and faith.

My Higher Power goes everywhere with Me. This Source is with Me in the grocery store, in My meetings, and in My sessions. I pray that My HP helps Me see what I'm supposed to see and do what I'm supposed to do. It's like Source and I are on a bicycle. Source steers. I just keep pedaling.

Feeling safe, I proceeded with My sessions and within seconds from their knock, My client could hear the sound of My heels coming closer to the door. Their thoughts were spinning rapidly while the crack of the door increased to reveal exactly who they met on the website and talked to on the phone. I was real. I was 100% real. And I stood before them like the Goddess they'd only dreamed of.

My studio was located in an edgy part of town in an old tire factory that'd been converted into working studios. My 1,200-square-foot unit had an open ceiling, exposed ductwork, and concrete floors throughout. Off to the side I had a little living room set up with a fuzzy white rug, leather couch, chair and a coffee table in between, which is where O/our previous phone conversation would resume. Around a makeshift bedroom was My bondage table, My spanking bench, and two very large armoires filled with all My goodies such as paddles, restraints, nipple clamps, and of course, panties, and dresses. Little did anyone know, the studio was also My home. I was on a very restricted budget, and affording another place was totally out of the question . . . at least at the time.

Within minutes of being in My presence, I asked the gentleman to have a seat upon My leather couch. Just the essence of My demeanor was enough for him to know who was in charge. I would take a seat in the leather chair across from them. They in no way had earned the privilege of sitting close to Me; the closest they would get at this point was an invitation to sit at My feet.

No matter the tone of My voice or the severity of My requests, My clients always knew they were never to be harmed. Uncomfortable, yes. But harmed, never. They came to Me to experience something they had never experienced before; perhaps a fantasy come to life or a grueling need that had never been fulfilled. No matter what the request or the apparatus I chose, the bottom line was that they were there to please Me.

During O/our time together, they would willingly follow My lead into various degrees of submission. Each step took them further and further from the realities of their outside demands. In My world, there was no such thing of judgment or worries of what another would think. Instead, it was a beautiful exchange of power guided by the feminine force. It was quite fulfilling for both of U/us. Something that would have them craving for more.

What many women misunderstand is the thrill men get from a strong, confident woman who knows what She wants, and truly enjoys getting it. Men function through the feeling of pride.

They have attributes such as strength, power, and competitiveness. So, to have a self-assured woman who is comfortable challenging these characteristics can be very electrifying for him. It can also be very fulfilling to express the opposite emotions.

Something that I am very comfortable doing.

CHAPTER FIFTEEN

Dominating Dogma

When we consider "domination," our head goes straight to the dominatrix because we don't know any other variables under that umbrella. When you hear the word dominatrix, you can already feel something happening within yourself. You feel a shift in your attention. Perhaps a shiver runs down your back. Even the 'x' at the end of the word feels dark, black, and final. A dominatrix is dressed in severe black or red; cold; there is no emotion during the scene. In fact, objectification is usually the goal of a dominatrix session, which is why we have all the apparatuses in a dungeon to create such a severe environment. It's dark with chains. Whips. Leather. Instruments of torture.

On the opposite end of the spectrum was My position as a FemDom. I was kind. Nurturing. Loving. An active facilitator in helping men express their inner desires. I taught My submissives how to be better husbands. I taught them how to better serve the higher gender. Just like in recovery, we have all different stories, but it's the feelings that unify us; it's the unmet yearning inside of us we all understand. I know what it's like to need something and not be able to ask for it. I know what it feels like to be in a relationship where My love and My heart are wide open and people on the outside disregard it and say that it's shameful.

When you shift that feeling of malaise, that inability to be understood or to be true to yourself into this dynamic, you can understand how My subs found such relief under My tutelage. Most men are carrying the weight of tremendous expectations, whether self-inflicted or as a product of society. The oppression of gender roles, religious expectations, and dogma overwhelms them.

He's a statue. He's gotta be big. He's gotta be strong. He's gotta be productive. He's gotta provide.

Underneath the facade, My submissives lived another life. He could not dream of telling his wife that he needed to relinquish some of the power that he had. He didn't know how to ask to be dominated. The freedom can be overwhelming to men, when all My clients wanted to do was ask, "Can you physically bind me to the bed so I have that kind of restriction or restraint? I don't want to move. I want to fight against something I can't break through. Life is too easy. I want resistance!"

I went through all of those stages, so I knew how to provide that space for them. I've been bound — psychologically, emotionally, mentally, physically. I know what it feels like to rage against confines I cannot break. When I was in love with Stacey — who transitioned to Adam — it was the most beautiful, authentic connection I'd ever experienced. Yet our same-sex love was unacceptable to others. When I arrived on the other side, I carried the gift of knowing how to simulate the same experience for My clients. What I did was provide experiences that few knew how to tune in and explore.

We blindfold people so we can take humanity out of the experience and go into the psychological aspects of what they're experiencing. My subs wanted to know what it felt like to be bound so they could fight unsuccessfully against the restraints. Internally, they went through a delicious cycle of relinquishing. When they finally got to where they stopped fighting, it would often bring them to tears. It felt so good to not be in charge. Not to be in control. That was the *crème de la crème* of the dynamic.

I learned early in my life that the monogamous lifestyle that people are often programmed to accept was not for Me. And naturally, I saw the same realization in My clients. Monogamy provides a set of expectations, including the notion that one person can meet all of your needs. You can see how these relationships can be set up to fail, as we are complex beings with a variety of desires. It's rare that one person can meet every need of another. I understood this implicitly, and the CEO who spent time with Me expected that I could provide an outlet for a part of him that he couldn't get in his primary relationship.

He couldn't ask his wife to meet him where he wanted to be seen. He couldn't share his desires with his friends or colleagues or golf partners. Yet he had other parts of himself that he felt called to express. Sometimes these men cultivated relationships with mistresses, but even then they were not feeling fully expressed. These relationships and these spaces that I provided offered a safe space for courage and authenticity. W/we developed a relationship between U/us that had nothing to do with marriage, children, wealth, financial support, or sex. It was a psychological partnership. A journey of self-exploration.

The beautiful thing about My position was that it was a combination of everything I ever wanted to be: a helper and a teacher. Through My work, Source helped Me come awake to My own creativity. I enjoyed writing and flipping the script. I was the writer, director, and heroine of My own studio. And My audience loved Me.

I know My clients felt comfortable with Me because they never refused My orders. And I understood why. As a sensitive, intuitive woman, I could sense the limits of others; I knew how far to push, and when to relent. Because O/our time together was a dynamic engagement, I was sensitive to limitations, the word no, and the need to stop. I have found the most liberating feeling is holding all the power and never violating others with it; every time I could take from another, and choose instead to heal them, I redeemed My childhood, and I served the other person. In a sense, I was an energy worker, and My studio was a place of release.

I've had men cry when they spent time with Me, because I knew how to push them to their limit. They did what I wanted them to do because it was Me they were there to please. Their submission was their gift to Me. O/our exchange was not about them, no matter the task. The motive behind O/our activities was all about My pleasure. So when they knew and understood that, they knew that no matter what, if I wanted them to suck on My feet, or lick My shoes — it didn't matter what it was — they were doing it to please Me.

I turned some clients away afterwards because I didn't like the energy they had generated between U/us. It didn't matter what I didn't like, if I didn't like it then it would not happen again. If O/our session went well, I might take them on and train them outside of My studio and direct them what to do from afar. I would completely encapsulate their world with thoughts of Me and My kinky ways. I might tell them, "Every day you've got to check in with Me at three o'clock. *My time*. Not your time. If you're in London, you better wake up and text Me that you're just checking in."

I had one gentleman named Bernard that I called bernadine. I called him and said, "bernadine, you need to go get your toes painted, sweetie. I love pink nail polish."

"Oh, Ma'am, I don't think that's a wise thing to do in my Southern town."

"You're arguing with Me. So now, on top of the pink nail polish, I want a little flower painted on your big toenail. You should probably stop arguing with Me right now."

"Yes, Ma'am." So off he went to get his toenails painted pink. The little Asian women were speaking their language and giggling. He called and said, "Ma'am, I think they're laughing at me."

"I hope they are, bernadine. I hope they're laughing real hard at you. Do you think they know you're wearing women's panties under your jeans right now?" I specialized in that sort of humiliation that would just tip the guys over. They loved it. bernadine served Me for many years. One time I shaved a big 'b' in his chest hair. It was fabulous. He had a girlfriend who was off to college, so there was the stress that she might make a surprise visit and see what I had done.

When he attended a fetish ball with Me, W/we were in a hotel and I had him locked up in a chastity cage. I said, "bernadine, you've got three minutes to find something within this hotel to cut that tab and get that cage off. Cause if you don't get it off in three minutes, it's going to stay on for another thirty days." he was running around like mad to do as I said, and he loved every minute.

My clients absolutely loved the idea that I was in control as they tired of the power seat in their everyday lives. That was the difference between My earlier years and stepping into My power as a FemDom. My clients were sober, consenting adults. Me too; I only did what they requested of Me, and only if I too wanted that level of exchange. With each playful humiliation and lick of My red-bottomed shoes, My past fell further and further into the rearview mirror.

And the men enjoyed the protocol. W/we ramped up until about 30 minutes before the session was going to end, then we had the climax and they would have to do exactly as they agreed. For example, I might tell a client that he had exactly three minutes to complete orgasm. When they went through the ramping up of having an orgasm, once they released, they shifted into an entirely different headspace. As they were catching their breath, the endorphins flooded their system. They would relax and want to take a nap, the sexual high dissipated. So I would play with that, too. I would remind them of O/our agreement: what came out must go back in.

Oh, you think it's all fun and games when you're turned on? I'll show you what true dominance is. You're going to have an orgasm and you're going to put it in this cup.

Now, they would be in a completely masculine mindset to start. But they would sober up from the sex high quickly when I'd direct various tasks with their ejaculate thereafter. They might have to fill an ice cube tray, freeze their semen and make little lollipops. Or I might pop a little straw in that cup and tell them they're going to finish what we started right that minute.

I did My part and now you have to do your part. Suck it up!

For clients that transitioned to remote services, I would later direct them when to eat their popsicles. They loved it because nobody ever humiliated them like that. They enjoyed My authoritative tone when I said, "You better be ready to suck on your popsicle. It's Friday and it will happen today when I text you to do so."

In the studio, I would leave them on the note that I might invite them back. It was not a given. There was nothing within My world that was a given. When they said, *Oh, Ms. Jewels, when can I see you again?* I would say that I would let them know.

"Just because you come in here one time doesn't mean that you have an open invitation," I'd say.

They walked out My door in a very vulnerable position. Very uncomfortable. Their pride was all up in arms as they experienced tremendous mental conflict. *Oh my God, that was the best thing I've ever done. Did I really do that? What if my friends ever knew I did that? How did She get me to do that? How could She do that to me?*

Because this was a relationship, it was dynamic, as all relationships are. Just as with any other relationship, each time W/we engaged together, W/we evolved a little more. This evolution changed both of U/us, and the relationship continued to flourish, which ultimately became even better than the first time.

I would have an idea of their budget, but typically if I desired it, My clients would see Me on a rotation of about once a month. Some exchanges were not full scenes. Perhaps they wanted to meet for coffee or do a foot fetish/foot rub, which required far less effort on My part. For a smaller scene, I could see them once every week or two. But I was not interested in doing a full-blown scene on the regular. This space was also better for the clients, who typically loved to build it up in their minds until O/our next encounter.

CHAPTER SIXTEEN

~/|\~

Tell Me Your Safe Word

According to the clients I have known, the type of interest I serve raises its head around puberty. Through listening to the secrets whispered to Me by many men, I've probed and investigated the things they enjoyed. Many have shared similar stories with Me, although the details varied. When they were going through puberty, they would steal their brother's porno magazines, go under a tent they'd made on their bed, turn on their flashlight and flip through the magazines while exploring their bodies.

On TV, they were watching Catwoman — clad in a revealing black latex bodysuit — tie up Batman. Between magazines and TV, these sorts of visuals were very stimulating to sexually awakening adolescent males. This is when they'd eventually figure out they enjoyed stealing their mom's nylons and tying their arms and legs together.

My clients admitted to having known about their interests since their early days of innocent exploration. They also knew, however, that they were *not supposed to* explore in that way. Something about it was shameful, so heaven forbid they talk to their buddies about it. Women are often privileged enough to graduate into talking about everything from vibrators to bodily fluids with each other, but outside of locker room talk, men don't have a safety net. Especially in the years they discover their sexuality; men learn to repress their urges; they feel they must keep their inner persona to themselves.

Mothers in Mom's generation tended to prim and proper, clad in clickety-clack high heels and nylons. Mothers were a source of love, so when I wrapped my arms around mom's legs as a little tyke, I experienced nylons and heels. When Mom walked in a room, she was clicking those heels as I turned my head to get her attention. And because they were once innocent children exploring the energy of the other sex, many men developed foot fetishes around their early days with their mothers — particularly high heel foot fetishes.

As My website specifically disclosed that I was a FemDom, the boys who sought Me out already understood My specific niche of discipline and humiliation. They enjoyed that motherly female figure looming over them, while reliving the thrill of Mom's psychological discipline. Mom told them what to do and how to behave with just a look in her eye. There was so much power there, and when I incorporated discipline and humiliation with some physicality, W/we would reach the full effect.

I enjoyed spanking, discipline, and authoritarianism, so I was an active participant in My exchanges with My clients. Some FemDoms and Dominatrixes are in it for the show, but I didn't feel that was a full energy exchange, although that works for some people. As W/we each progress at different levels, some clients sought to delve much deeper into the psychological aspect of our exchanges. It thrilled Me to meet them there.

Knowing what I knew, when a man came into My arena, he felt so vulnerable, all of his secret parts exposed. His defenses were down around his feet. I'd ask questions of him about his early explorations with sex. *When was the first time you masturbated? What were some of your earliest kinks? When was the first time you went into your mom's underwear drawer? Did you put on her nylons? Or did you bind yourself with them?*

If I agreed to see a man, he knew he had to provide Me with the financial aspect of O/our exchange for My time. I was the provider; they held reverence for My being the alpha. They understood the time factor since they were lawyers, CEOs, or doctors — men in positions of power. I also made sure I was receiving something for My energy, which is how I cared for Myself. Our relationships were more than time, money, or business on My end. When I asked them to paint their toenails, that was for Me, and I refused to take on clients who did not understand this; I had needs and desires as well; they had to understand that they were satisfying their Ma'am and Her spoken requests.

Reestablishing power with men that ruled the world gave Me a sense of leverage with My demons. Though I had worked through most of them in recovery, the wounded inner child in Me lived on. For My entire life, I had been a dancing puppet for masculinity. Now, I was the puppeteer — and My clients wanted to submit to Me. In O/our exchanges, they did not see Me as another obligation, nor something else they had to do. I did not demand an emotional connection, which was often one of their biggest struggles. I wasn't asking for obligations moving forward; I asked only for the fun. My clients saw O/our experiences as a reward rather than another demand to tick off the list.

Most, if not all, of My clients didn't tell their wives what they needed. However, there was one incident of a gentleman who left his email open and his wife learned of his interests. She read through O/our exchanges and became desperate to provide this experience for her husband. She was an executive's wife who lived in a protected world, so while she was not worldly, she wanted to meet her husband's needs, but didn't know how to use her own power to accommodate him.

She tried to be a dominant woman who could humiliate her husband. But to pull off this exchange, she would have had to have been Dominant. She would have had to have been comfortable grabbing the reins and going for it. She did her best, but she didn't have the skills or experience. One of the chief complaints I would hear from my clients, as they would relate to me scenarios similar to this that they'd experienced, was that it wasn't real. And such was the case here; the executive's wife was just trying to play a role, and wasn't able to make it authentic enough.

It wasn't only in My studio where I was a dominant part of My clients' lives. I very much enjoyed working remotely and asking them questions such as, "What did you do for your wife today? Did you rub her feet? Did you soak her in the bath?" Or perhaps I'd say, "This Saturday, you're going to wash the car and take the trash out without being asked. And you cannot come back in and tell her what you did. Just do it without appreciation." And the men would eat it up.

Unless I had a submissive in My space, My dominant side was not fully activated. Since I understood that shift, I subsequently knew that My men enjoyed being submissive in the safety of My studio when W/we played together. Once they were back home without Me, I encouraged them to engage their submissive energy to draw out the dominant energy of their partner. His wife may not have been aware of what was happening and just enjoyed being pampered. I encouraged drawing out the side of her that was uncomfortable. In a 15-year marriage, she might very much enjoy the shift and feel safe enough to say to her husband, "I want you to wash my car again next Saturday. And I'd like another foot rub while you're at it."

Many ask how FemDoms can take advantage of men through FinDomming, for example. The answer would be that I don't get the enjoyment of the mummification fetish. I don't understand it, but I can provide it, although it's not something I enjoy. I can put any service in the same category, because it is something I am providing and to offer My services. There has to be a consenting consumer. Whether the exchange involves human burial or stapling the testes or sending money to a face on the internet, it's between adults. It's not taking advantage of anyone, in fact I would argue that it is liberating them by adding value and demonstrating freedom.

Some may not understand My job, which is to take a man who's successful in socially acceptable ways, and encourage his self-exploration in the less understood ways. That's what he comes to see Me for; that's why he enjoys paying for the experience with

Me. If you don't understand such an exchange, then your perception is likely through the eyes of a woman. Perhaps you have fears such as I'm taking advantage of My clients. I'm misleading them. I'm hurting them. I find this perspective is usually harbored by women because of internal issues and insecurities they have not worked through. So much of this concern is the shadow side of feminine energy; it's wounding from the past that creates this misperception.

If we turn the scenario around, we often see a big, strong provider who is providing for his partner. He gives gifts for the feeling that he gets in return. The woman in his life performs her roles for the feelings she gets from him. The energetic exchange in any relationship is based on the feeling of giving. I go to a movie to get scared or to laugh or to cry. I pay a ticket for the experience. And then I go home. Just because I cry at the movie does not mean that the actor is a terrible person because they played the villain, evoking a sad response from me. I'm going to the movies for the experience and to feel something, and that's how this works as well. They are paying for something to unlock their senses and emotions; sometimes it means more than that, sometimes it doesn't. Either way, it's their personal desire and request, so I deliver.

The world of domination is ever-changing, there are always generation gaps, and We in the business try to grow with the times. I strive to understand those younger than Me; I accept I may never. In My generation, the yin and the yang were prevalent in our various rituals. We had a lot of practice whereas the newer culture doesn't have that. Now women put up a post and ask a multimillionaire to give them money for their hair or a fancy dinner. You might think, *But you're just a kid. How can you just ask men to give you money?* I think it's part of that evolution as well, but Mine is definitely more of that. I'm so grateful that I got to do the dance of high heels and stockings, as that's definitely My era.

The one thing all generations in this community have in common is that we were young once. We all processed the tension of whether we were going to go work at McDonald's, or work on the pole. We all chose the pole. Well, maybe both for a while. But I would like to see My generation create a space of safety for younger girls. Men have been driven like this forever; it started with *Playboy* and *Penthouse*. But women are the ones who are questioned. There needs to be an eradication of shame on both sides, a coming to center between being rendered powerless and aggression. I've certainly always oscillated between being silent and screaming from the rooftops; I think there's value in My generation teaching the younger in a way that is also open to being taught.

It helps to have maternal figures as mentors in the business when things go awry, and trust Me, they do. I've had experiences with clients that didn't go quite the way they should have during the session. I am pretty decent at reading people; I sensed it was a case of the male ego as opposed to misreading My client. Often, when male clients come in, they want Me to be proud of them. Instead of using their safe word, RED!, they will endure more than they wish in order to make Me feel proud. It's hard to bear; to give someone 20 more swats with a paddle when I see their bodies are speaking loudly. When I see them reach this point out of ego, I have to put an end to O/our session. I will not take part in an act that harms, and I hurt that some of these men are out to harm themselves because of their pride.

There are no consequences to saying RED. When I encounter clients of this nature, I say, "You should have called orange or yellow three swats ago, but you didn't. So as a disciplinarian, I am going to show you what happens when you don't do as you're told. I told you that you should have called yellow when it was time. Now, we have to stop."

Nothing ever went completely astray in My studio. I wanted My clients to trust Me no matter what, because in My arena, I knew best. This required My commitment to learning them even if they were not self-aware. I would notice how their body was responding; I would catch what was right or wrong by the way it was reacting. So never did things go south, because the client usually got to where he would learn to call RED, and if they didn't, I would. Most men are not in touch with their bodies because they haven't been living authentically, so it's possible they might not know when to call yellow. In the beginning, I wouldn't have known either, because of the dissociation I experienced prior to My addiction. I watch for this, both as an energy healer and someone who has lived it.

There is a common belief that those of us who felt they had no control as a child grow up with the burning desire to have control and take it out on men because men were the ones who hurt us. I find this a reductive, stereotypical projection. When the things that happened to Me took place, Source was right alongside Me, caring for My energetic body amid pain. I believe Source has always been by My side, especially in the terrible times.

The healing process I underwent took place in the invisible landscape of the human soul. Man could not judge nor measure it. When I received hugs from the women in the ICU waiting room after Mom had her lung removed, I connected with Source at My core and I understood the breadth of supernatural provision and care. I've learned that when I experienced things like that, I was being healed. For some, it is unfathomable to believe healing can take place in a dungeon, or in My studio. But it is what certain individuals need on their healing journeys. Me included. Together, we heal in areas we didn't even realize needed light until they are exposed.

All throughout My life I'd been healing. It was a gradual, erratic process as opposed to one moment in time. It's a spectrum, as we are always healing on many levels at once. Because of this, I believe My current identity has nothing to do with My trauma as a child. That little girl is healed.

The abilities I used in the domination space with other individuals were a product of the evolution of healing My psychological self. It comes solely from a place of love and nurturing. I've harmed nobody. I may have had different apparatuses to invoke this emotion or that reaction, but that wasn't the drive behind eliciting experiences. I was providing space for somebody who could not be a hundred percent authentic in their real world — the sole reason I was called to FemDom.

CHAPTER SEVENTEEN

Going International

Sobriety enabled Me to step into My power and My calling. For the first time in My life, I could be free to kick back and enjoy My life. And I was having a hell of a lot of fun. Men were loving Me and I was finally making substantial money with My Source-given gifts. As I was in charge, the relationships between Me and My clients were non-sexual, which empowered Me in all the ways I had always needed and deserved. Each experience allowed Me yet another advance up the rungs toward enlightenment.

Then *he* applied.

Although I had received hundreds of applications, as I read Andrew's, a smile played at the corners of My lips. According to his answers, I could see that W/we were an immediate match. Like Me, he was interested in bondage, humiliation, and worship. He lived in Belgium, so I could enjoy O/our time together without worrying about him showing up at My front door with his suitcases.

I emailed and told him I would call Thursday at two o'clock. He knew the drill and responded that he would be available. I got a good feel for him on O/our phone call. He had taken the time to make sure he was alone without interruptions. Andrew took direction well and easily answered My intimate questions.

W/we set up a time for his visit within the week to take advantage of that initial ramp-up period. He met Me at the dungeon where I played with him for two hours. Afterward, W/we met several more times; each experience building upon the session before. In the beginning of our relationship, I said, "You need to go back home to Belgium." But then Andrew visited more often, and O/our communication increased outside of O/our sessions together. Uh oh. This wasn't how this was supposed to go!

Then I got the call. "I want you to come to Belgium for two weeks."

"I can't afford to do that. You can't just call Me up and buy Me. Absolutely not," I said.

The nerve!

"Well," he said, undeterred, "I'm going to give you My debit card to make the arrangements. And Ms. Rita is invited to come out for one week on My dime." Despite My reservations, he offered anything and everything I demanded. So, Ms. Rita and I traveled to Belgium and a good time was had by all during O/our time together. A few days after I returned to the States, I got the next call, "I've asked my wife for a divorce."

Double uh-oh. Triple uh-oh.

Now, Ms. Rita had said to Me more than a couple of times, "Jewels, never let them get so caught up in you that they leave their wives. That's the power you have as a FemDom. You're beautiful and you have the balls to tell them what to do. You're that powerful. The exchange is addicting for them and they will want more and more and more because finally that spot inside them is being fulfilled."

Well, Ms. Rita was right. And since Andrew could afford to have Me live with him full time, I accepted his offer and moved to Belgium for a year. As I began making preparations to leave, I realized this latest move wasn't as simple as the days when I had thrown My belongings in black garbage bags and hit the road. This time, I had to dissolve My household, which was considered damaging to the boys who dedicated themselves to Me. This was the first time in My life that I couldn't just run down the road and not concern Myself with those I left behind.

As I'd made commitments to the boys in My household, setting them free was a big deal emotionally. It also was a big deal within the community, and I lost some credibility in the scene because of the way I handled My dissolution. The dynamic between a Ma'am and Her boy is like a marriage. As the head of the household, I was the One who made sure My boys were okay. I ensured they were taking care of their bodies by eating well and going to the gym, for example.

My boys had a great level of dependence upon My direction, and when I dissolved My household, I took that away from them. Of course they were functioning men outside of O/our relationship and they were going to be just fine, but My announcement sent them into a tailspin. *What do I do? Where do I go? What am I supposed to do next?*

According to the standard and accepted protocol within the community, when I dissolved a relationship, I was supposed to hand off My boys to someone else who would observe them during the process of O/our separation. If I were to remain in the area at the dissolution, then I would have been responsible for making sure they landed in a new situation and became stable. Just as when I met david, he was under the responsibility of another who transferred his protection to Me. My responsibility was to remain present to help them transition.

My departure for Belgium created a mark on My name; I took a hit in the lifestyle community. However, I enjoyed many of the people in the community, but when it came down to it, they weren't the ones who paid My bills. For some people, the opinions of others are big game-changers. Not for Me. Ms. Jewels was going international. I had no time at all for pandering to people with small capacities.

During My time in Europe, I met with Mistress Anya of Other World Kingdom, a small city in the Czech Republic completely ruled by women. OWK is a private state, founded upon the principle of a slave-holding Matriarchal monarchy. According to their website, The OWK is governed on the basic principle that the WOMAN is always, everywhere and in everything superior to the male creature! Established in 1580, the queendom has a national flag and a coat of arms.

Mistress Anya was one woman who belonged to OWK, so I became her apprentice. She showed Me what a true BDSM Dominatrix was. I would do sessions with her at her in-home studio and see amazing Japanese rope bondage called *shirbari*. She was a true Dominatrix who provided all the extreme pleasures her clients were seeking.

Soon I was delighted to attend different events with her. In Europe, they do everything to the nines and I saw some of the most wildest things — including a horse on a boat in Paris, France. One gentleman, opposed to just wearing a halter and leads, wore a full black latex horse suit, replete with hooves and a hood with horse ears. I smiled to Myself. I'd come a long way since My early days in a small town in the Midwest.

In retrospect, I see I fooled Myself into believing I was in Belgium solely as an act of service. Despite externally resisting it, I fell in love for the first time in My life. I was being received, and I was receiving. I was smitten with Andrew and W/we enjoyed a glorious year together. Then his wife found out about Me and she prepared to hightail it back to Belgium with their daughter in tow. I think his disclosure about Me was intentional because I don't think he had the guts to tell her the truth. W/we had to sanitize the apartment in Belgium to prepare for her impassioned return.

As W/we scrubbed and cleaned and laundered, Andrew insisted that he wasn't going anywhere. He said he had to figure out the situation with his wife and daughter and that he couldn't get a divorce in Belgium. Now, I was still practicing My program of recovery and I heard in meditation that I could take care of Myself. And so, despite the unexpected upheaval and the race to sanitize the apartment of every trace of Me, I held My head high amongst the heartbreak, knowing that somehow I was going to be okay.

On a cool spring morning, Andrew and I said our goodbyes,

and I stoically boarded my plane to fly from Belgium to our state — as his wife and daughter flew from our state to Belgium. We probably passed in the skies, something I thought about as I gazed out the airplane window, chewing on my fingernail.

I arrived back in the city that was to be our home with great hope, excited for Andrew's imminent return where we were going to be together. I had no doubts about our future. I was certain we would figure everything out. Dreaming of the magic we experienced in Belgium, I looked at apartments in uptown, imagining us together as I scrolled through the different floor plans.

With Andrew's encouragement, I chose an upscale apartment that ran what was then a steep $1,300 a month for me considering I had no job and I had no clientele. I had given my all and came back from Belgium with nothing. Andrew put $10,000 into my bank account to get the apartment started, and I was still full-blown in the reality that this was going to happen. IKEA delivered new furniture that weekend. Not being in a position to pay a monthly bill, I got a TracFone, loading minutes to use it when I could.

I moved in and soon started working in a house that was converted to an exquisite dungeon. The walls were dark purple with black furnishings — which included a gyno chair, full medical room with a hospital bed, and many other instruments of torture. Despite the more than ample setup, my heart wasn't in it.

I didn't yet have enough money for a car, and then Andrew told me he couldn't send any more because he didn't want his wife to find out. Winter was blowing across Minneapolis, and so lacking a vehicle of my own, I had to take the bus to the less desirable parts of Minneapolis for appointments with my clients. I dressed in boots to my knees, trekking through snowbanks to get to the city bus, carrying Ms. Jewels in my backpack.

Thanksgiving was the date when Andrew had said he would leave his wife, but the holiday came and went with no word from him. I picked at congealed stuffing and cold turkey breast from the restaurant down the street, and watched the Macy's Day Parade on TV. I believed him when he said he was coming. He probably just ran into a snag or two and would be on the next plane. I just knew it!

After that, I continued to count days. I counted weeks. I counted moments, dreaming of our grand reunion. I wanted to believe that the feelings were there. But I believe that he had a lot going on in his career that took up most of his headspace. Emotions were not his strong suit, nor was handling a failing marriage. Still, I remained hopeful. Surely he would arrive soon.

Since Andrew couldn't send any more money, I took a part-time job at a hospital in the surgery, juggling life as a mistress by day and working in the hospital at night. Then came the pivotal moment. There has always been something that triggers me into sheer terror when I'm in a dark space by myself, and I can't see the world around me. One night, I got out of work at 7:00 p.m., and I was sitting in a shelter waiting on a bus; it was dark, I was alone, and it was bitterly cold.

It was like this voice screamed in my head: *How did I get here?* And that was it, when I realized that something had to change. I had a talk with my sponsor, Anita, who was with me every step of the way. She said, "Jewels, the writing is on the wall."

"What are you talking about?"

"He's not coming back."

"Andrew is coming back. Soon we'll be together again."

"You're living in a fantasy. He doesn't have the courage. He doesn't have the balls. He is not strong enough for you. Maybe his wife gave him an ultimatum that he needed to cut everything off with you," she continued.

I knew she meant well, but people can be wrong. I trusted her judgment, but I just couldn't believe that was true. Then the day finally arrived for Andrew to return to our city to work. I had spent hours — well, to be honest, months — preparing for our grand reunion. He arrived on time, and spent the entire afternoon with me, soaking up the affection I so willingly gave. And then, as he was walking out, he turned back and called over his shoulder, "I can't do this anymore." And he exited my life without turning around even once.

I stood in the half-furnished apartment that I couldn't afford and felt my entire body collapse. The life washed right out of me in such a rush, if my soul had exited my body, it would not have surprised me. I was shocked almost to death. However, I put on my poker face, the one I had so much experience wearing. I had no intention of being the melting, sappy girlfriend to Andrew, so I put up a front.

Ms. Jewels is all about love. She is meant to love and comfort and heal people. And sexuality is the biggest sore that needs love. And I needed it desperately right then; it'd been yanked out from beneath me without a warning. I got through that first day, reminding myself that I was strong. I had been through worse. I would get through this, too.

I saw that although I was sober, and in recovery, I was emotionally relapsing. And when I confronted the reality that Andrew was not coming back, I couldn't hold it together. My poker face mask fell off, clattering on the floor. One moment I would be in CVS, looking at hairspray, while the next moment found me in a puddle blowing bubbles. I knew that my decision-making was skewed and began taking those steps to crawl back out of the hole I'd dug myself into.

Recovery had taught me to make changes day by day, and so I did just that until the lease was up. Alone with myself, I recognized that I'd been waiting for Andrew for a year, but I had nothing to show for it but a TracFone. I didn't have a car. I had a half-furnished apartment with IKEA furniture. I was swinging a paddle in some ghetto. I made the decision to move back to the big city in the spring once the lease was up.

There are absolutely no mistakes. Every situation has a lesson to be learned, so I let Andrew go. But he wasn't the only loss on the horizon. Ms. Rita had been in my life for many years; but our relationship was fated. We would attend private parties, conferences and workshops within the same community, but we would eventually lose touch. Sadly, she ended up relapsing, and we never spoke again. The last time I saw her at a charity event, she looked like she was struggling. I was sad to let go of someone I once admired. But I was used to goodbyes.

CHAPTER EIGHTEEN

Big Fish

I returned to the big city and re-established myself in the community, stronger than ever. I placed ads and men contacted me through my website. They answered my standard questions about lifestyle, family, logistics, and preferences. I made it clear I wanted no love-struck fools ending up at my front door with their suitcases.

The immediate success felt like a baptism; an affirmation that I was doing the right thing. I'm not an egotistical person, so I didn't measure my success around how many men I had in my stable. But I was aware of what I was worth, and thriving in my natural gifts felt deliciously affirming. I poured all of my energy into the one-on-one exchanges I shared with each of my clients. Their trust rejuvenated me, giving me confidence in my intuition and ability to transcend the scene. The safety that men felt when they came into my space convinced me that I was where I belonged.

I praised the fact that I'm emotionally mature. If something were to go south, I knew I could handle anything. I will not freak out. I will not call the cops. I knew what to do in any situation. This gave me an invaluable sense of confidence in those transactions that many will never know. Some people never learn how to take up space in their bodies and lives. After overcoming the lows of physical and emotional boundary violations, I knew my beginnings and my ends; I knew where my *"NO!"* lived, and I called the shots.

My time in recovery taught me the value of living embodied. Through energy work, I've been able to discern others who are not as self-aware, and spur them into better understanding of themselves. The male anatomy needs care in a way that differs from the female anatomy.

Women enjoy textiles, lotions, and soft things that feel good on our skin. Men don't have that same sort of sensitivity to their body. That's why they can endure more on a physical level. When a woman sees someone in a hood, with their privates locked up in a black charity cage, it can appear to be frightening. They might interpret it as the most terrifying thing a man could experience. But my men found it tantalizing and enjoyed their power being challenged.

Some men enjoy the endorphin rush that pain gifts. If a part of their body is pinched, such as a nipple, it goes numb quickly. The discomfort comes when I release the pinch and the blood flushes through the numb spot. The endorphins are the resultant pleasure. Along with the endorphin rush, I let them wear that secret hat they had desired for so long.

You're locked up, and only I hold the key. There's nothing you can do to change the outcome. There's no harm done. Submit. Just submit. No one will know.

My own fulfillment, besides the currency, was the exchange itself. While the currency was certainly attractive, I prided myself on putting a lot of my being into every exchange. I enjoyed bringing fantasies to life; like when you're watching a movie, daydreaming about the most attractive character. I was able to play that out for people, and it was creative for them and for me. I created an energy and a newness they could bottle inside and take home until our next visit. I taught them how to reveal an aspect of themselves they'd blissfully explore, not dissimilar to the way Source revealed FemDom to me. This release is why I was chosen for this calling.

I recognize that some people will feel uncomfortable with my referring to it as a calling, but the more I reiterate the truth, the more it is dignified as such. The world needs to be challenged beyond the precipice of their understanding and their beliefs. Not all kinks, or seemingly darker avenues of sexuality, are derived from trauma. The number one question people ask dominant women is, were you abused as a child? Initially, I found this question frustrating because the questioner wouldn't even know my given name; nor who I was on the inside. Why were they assuming something as grave as that? But I always handled my response with grace, and perhaps unnecessary self-punishment for the impropriety; a byproduct of socialized shame that I am always actively unwiring.

None of us have shame in our minds as children. I didn't — even in the earliest years of my sexual abuse. It developed over time. In seediness. In darkness. In secrecy. The dirty feelings surrounding what I had endured only came into my awareness when I learned about societal appropriateness regarding sex. Western, shame-based religions influence much of this, so even if I hadn't been molested, I wouldn't have been spared from the indoctrination; that I was repeatedly assaulted just adds insult to injury. It was too much for my young mind to process.

All of my work in recovery was to dismantle shame so that it would no longer have a place in my adult life. It gave my resiliency and vigilance a clean window to shine through. I did not grow up wishing to become an alcoholic, move all over the countryside, or humiliate men. That is not how I see my work, though I am acutely aware it is how the world might do so. It was Source that gave me the ability to discover myself and my abilities, and it is only because of Source that I am thriving exactly where I should be.

Western values have a maligned sense of sexuality, and an allegiance to misunderstanding the value of sex workers. They put everything from burlesque to dancing to BDSM under the same umbrella as prostitution and child trafficking. There is little opportunity to professionally represent the community, because those on the outside love to label us as heinous. Bringing dignity to sex work would save lives. Providing things like healthcare, protection, and fostering regulation would support those who feel called to it, and protect those who get into it for misguided reasons. If we dignified sex work as work, the entire culture of the United States would shift into a healthier space. It would remove taboo and liberate every gender in our culture.

Those who go into sex work from a place of empowerment are not the same as powerless people being victimized against their will. It perpetuates abuse to strip women of the right to own their bodies and professional activities — specifically those who have worked through trauma. Including those who've never expanded in their sexual identity in an empowering way.

Consensual sexuality can enlighten the masculine and the feminine, and energetically this is good. Did my abuse catalyze my healing journey that led me to exploring the power exchange and the higher existence of female domination? Yes. But that's the only way the two are connected. My interactions with my clients were always about free will; they peaked at the highest level of seduction I provided, and they paid for it. I never had sex with my clients; our exchanges were merely for the enjoyment of my client's eroticism and release.

What people do not understand about our line of work is that there is a disconnect, just like in any other professional setting. Arousal with clients was never a thing. I never got turned on by any part of these business exchanges; I only came awake for interests in my personal life, like Andrew, who kept things exciting, romantic, and hot. Only if I loved someone, would I open myself up to intimate connection. When I did, my energy felt like me and not Ms. Jewels. In my studio, I got a psychological thrill that was energetically off the charts, but after my client left, I did not miss him. I did not need him.

Men don't want to hear that. They want to believe that if they opened the door to sex that I was going to be dripping wet with anticipation and relief because he was. Well, I'm not wired that way. I kept my love and relationships separate from my professional life. I had to be mindful to always keep sexual allure in the forefront when interacting with my clients, but receiving a foot rub did not turn me on.

As I rebuilt my self-esteem after my relationship with Andrew ended, I took pleasure in growing my strength. I no longer witnessed yesteryear in my current life. I was determined to revel in the present moment and become who I was destined to be. I learned to trust the light beckoning to me, no matter how it appeared to others. At the end of each energetic exchange with my clients, I always felt positive and more whole. I trusted in that, no matter what.

The most exciting element of my business was that I never knew who was going to walk through the door. Just as Andrew had arrived unexpectedly, a very special gentleman came to see me a few times before he proposed the idea of being exclusive with him. In a condescending tone, my response was, "You can't afford me."

"Yes, I can," he quickly assured me.

And boy, could he. Bryan was a multi-millionaire with 25 years of sobriety and he soon made arrangements to have me all to himself.

He enjoyed the idea of me flying with him to the West Coast for his business engagements. Now I didn't bust out the latex and leather each night of our travels, because that wasn't what he was looking for. He desired more of the mentality behind our engagements. If he had a business dinner on an evening, I might call and tell him to stop by and pick up a particular thing on his way back to the hotel. I'd have a scene set up for his return.

If we went out to dinner together, I would either put him in panties, lock him up in a cage, or ask him to wear a butt plug under his fancy suit. We would enjoy our dinner at a steak restaurant, looking nice and dressed to the nines, and I would lean over and lovingly whisper, "How do those panties feel? Is that getting a little uncomfortable? Cause it thrills me that you're wearing that just for me."

As a gentleman that was used to being in the power seat, he

enjoyed the unexpected surprises of humiliation. For example, if the server put the check down before him, I would slide it toward me and say, "I don't allow him to handle the money. That's my department. I'm going to have to buy this one." Bryan's face would burn red with that subtle yet powerful humiliation. He loved having a woman take control. I didn't need to scream and yell and wear crazy costumes and beat him senseless. I didn't have to do any of that because my specialty is seduction and humiliation.

Bryan came from an abusive family. On the outside, he was highly successful, but on the inside he was a closeted trans-gender. Because of his station and familial arrangement, nobody could know his real self. I give him credit for figuring it out, and during our time together, I held space for him. Because wealth is currency, I asked to be taught in exchange. I said, "I don't want you to give me the fish, I need you to teach me how to fish. I don't want your handouts. Teach me, empower me."

And that is exactly what he did. He created an LLC, made me a partner, gave me a bank account, paid off my student loans, arranged for me to get braces, put me up in a high-rise condo, put me through real estate school. He also set me up with Vanguard, so I had a 401k.

I had arrived. I owned properties. I was an executive vice president of all, while empowering his secret and allowing him room to flourish. When I became a real estate agent and took a seat in that room, I reveled in a new kind of power. I looked around at a room full of equals. I had the same credentials as everybody else for the first time in my life. Sitting at that desk was all I'd ever wanted; I had reached the pinnacle of all that I had been wanting after working for my entire life. I wore heels. I lived in the high-rise. I was a corporate woman. I was proud. For a while.

I worked with his secretary. I signed the checks to his son when he worked during the summer. Bryan trusted me a hundred percent. I had access to all of his wealth. He wanted me to meet his wife, so she knew who I was, but I refused. I saw myself as somebody who provided a service — but I was not a family member. I loved Bryan as a person but I was not madly in love with him and lusting over him; it was a different kind of love.

When we traveled, Bryan would become Juliette. We'd go to foreign cities, where no one would recognize him. He enjoyed attending transgender conferences as Juliette, in the clothing and makeup he could not wear around his family or in his big city life. Finally, he started taking estrogen for himself, all while concealing his gender dysmorphia from his family.

Bryan was an angel that Source brought me, who elevated me into his financial bracket. Not only did he teach me everything I needed to know, he gave me all the proceeds from the properties and business we eventually sold. In return, I gave him the freedom to be seen for who he really was.

He was married with a family, yet no one really knew him. He couldn't share himself in his conservative zip code; he had to get out of town just to come home to himself. We were two hardcore, money-driven folks. We had a similar drive, so he trusted me with all of his bank accounts. I saw his wife's checking account. I saw consecutive zeros that I'd never seen on paper before, such as $30,000 in hotel expenses for a week in Hawaii. I came to learn it's great to have money, and to love money, but there are also things, amidst having money, that are more valuable than consecutive zeros. Bryan was invaluable to me.

There were so many beautiful things that happened through our connection. Now, if I would have taken the world's dogma and slapped it with a title, I would have been called a well-kept woman, a mistress, a home wrecker. But it was love. It was acceptance. Our exchange provided Bryan with the hope he needed to preserve his will to live. At 74 years of age, he was very brave to face himself in the mirror. Let's face it: a 74-year-old man in high heels is probably not runway material, but that didn't matter to us. I bought lower shoes, and we adapted to who he was, where he was.

My big fish and I were together for five years. It was always an exclusive relationship on my end. You might wonder how I felt about knowing he was deceiving his wife of many years, and that

I was a participant in that deception. Naturally, that thought has crossed my mind, but I know I was a service to Bryan, and my relationship with him served a purpose. I feel no need to defend something I'm certain was contractual in spirit — a responsibility I was born to uphold.

I learned in AA that I cannot control anything. To throw the mantle of blame on the mistress is taking the responsibility away from the married party. The marriage agreement was between Bryan and his wife. He chose to be unfaithful by the world's definition. He did it, knowing he was the one deciding. He did it because he knew Juliette deserved to live. And it was Bryan himself who explained this distinction to me.

My karma and my connection with Source were what I needed to concern myself with. Boundaries of marriage and relationship are human contracts. In my world, I loved more than one person, so to obligate me to one person went against the grain of my nature. If my purpose was to come into this world at this time frame and give love, it was not conditional on everything from calendars to time to contracts between people. That's just dogma: other people's way of containing the world and making it functional.

Although Bryan and I were together for five years, we were not together every day. He gave me a lot of space. I lived downtown. I'd go to the office. To the outside world, we were business partners. He was involved in real estate, and merging and acquisitions. He established a scholarship at a university for women with children and those going through gender transitions. I was their point of contact. They'd contact me to say, "I graduated and I couldn't have done this without you." But it wasn't me; it was Bryan supporting others like him behind the scenes. My angel had a heart of gold.

As the years passed, a startling reality eclipsed everything: I had everything I'd ever thought I wanted, but outside of the pride from the accolades, I was deeply unfulfilled. I lived in a three-quarter-of-a-million-dollar condo in the city with floor to ceiling windows. All my bills were paid. I was driving a Mercedes.

Everything, including my hair, was perfect. I had no reason to be miserable. But I was. I didn't feel... like me.

Where did I get this insight that this was supposed to be so amazing up here? Who told me this would be IT? Was it some television or movie show that promised me that this city would be super glamorous?

I took some time to consider my own vacancy and realized, when it's dark out, it's dark inside. I recognized an enormous gaping hole in my heart. I had no one left to love, and despite my fierce independence, that just didn't feel right.

I had done the full journey. I didn't die on the way. I got there. But where was "there"? *There* without love was nowhere. I was a new kind of lost, in a house that was too big for me, and in a circumstance in which I didn't want to be. So, I went back to the drawing board, knowing I had made a lifestyle out of rising like a phoenix from the ashes. My primary goal was to get back to myself, and find out what she really wanted. Even if it involved a set of black trash bags: I was ready.

CHAPTER NINETEEN

❤〜

Made for the Stage

It's easy to underestimate the BIG-small things that shape us
as children. It's even easier to dismiss how those ghosts
haunt us for decades to come. Because she was teased and
ridiculed by her father for her weight, my mom developed a
pretty significant body-image issue: body dysmorphia, we call it
today. Growing up, it was yet another one of those things we
never talked about directly. She'd twirl in front of us and mention her progress on the Atkins diet, and brag about how she'd
only eaten saltines that day. She trained us to praise her when
she looked pretty or had lost weight. We knew to applaud her
deprivation, lauding it as an accomplishment.

When I was in my twenties, Mom and I took a trip to Kohl's.
Because she was a bargain shopper, she didn't invest in items
outside of Goodwill. Old habits die hard, I guess. But for whatever reason, on this specific occasion, she'd decided to invest in
better clothing. We went in gung-ho, and I got my hopes up. I
was going to support my mom; we were going to connect; we
were going into this together. She had gained weight and was
terrified, so she dragged me along for support.

I reveled in my natural role, saying, "Don't worry. Don't even
look at the tags, I'll deal with them. You just try on what I hand
you."

"Jewels, I can't deal with an XL or an XXL on the tag."

"You don't have to. I will."

That appeased her, so together we picked out an assortment of clothes. She smiled at the colors and styles and eagerly tossed the different items into our cart. In the changing room, she first put on a body shaper, which is quite a process of squeezing excess rolls into a tight casing. By default, body parts push out everywhere, willy-nilly. It's just part of being a woman in the world. If you push this part in, it's going to squeeze out somewhere else. From the outside of the stall, I could hear her panting because of her effort to pull this on and squeeze into that. The sighs of frustration only grew louder as she went through all that effort and disliked the fluorescent-lit view in the mirror. She put so much effort into getting into the clothes that suddenly, she lashed out with frustration, shutting the entire experience down. Exiting the changing room, she angrily threw all 30 or so pieces of clothing back into the basket and very uncharacteristically, she muttered, "FUCK IT." And we walked out.

I'd put in so much effort to help Mom like her appearance, and I felt utterly deflated as we walked toward her car. This is just one example of what I witnessed my mom go through time and time again. She was always on some new diet or starvation program, but as she aged, her body refused to respond in the way it had when she was younger. The pounds accumulated as she got bigger when she entered her later fifties as she didn't exercise aside from walking.

We shared clothing for years. However, when I entered my twenties and thirties, her body changed and mine didn't. As evidence of her mindlessness around her physical weight, when she was in the ICU dying of cancer, her comment was that she would finally get back into those skinny jeans. And then I had my epiphany. Not even the rattle of death could shake her free of the terrible things she believed about herself.

I realized that I too was tired of all the effort I'd put into trying to find this perfection that I'd learned to seek. Like Mom in that dressing room, I became exhausted, trying to mold my body into the perfect shape. If I walked into a place with a high bar stool, I would purposely sit in the back so if I crossed my legs while wearing shorts or a skirt, nobody would see cellulite. My seat in the room was almost as big of a mental obsession as was any situation where somebody could see my body.

When leaving after having sex, I would never leave the room walking face out. I would do this little shimmy thing to hide myself. God forbid someone would ask me to shower with them because all of those tapes were playing in the back of my mind constantly.

Do a cellulite check after dressing in shorts.

Don't lean too far forward.

Make sure they hold the camera at a slightly above angle.

Dim the lights for sex.

When I was forty years old, I started meeting with a trainer at a corporate gym three times a week. We did the functional training and not a lot of weight training. I saw some changes in my body, a little less here and a little more there. Before the mirror, I flexed my arms and saw the definition taking place in my upper body. That was all I needed to see to feel inspired, so I hit my workouts even harder. More weights. Cardio, cardio, and more cardio. With each minor shift in my physique, I manifested a new goal: Thinner. Shapelier. Stronger. Fitter.

I was in a super vulnerable area with myself and when physically building your body, your form needs to be proper. So if I was to do a triceps push-down, I couldn't do it with hunched shoulders. My body understood we were supposed to stand up straight and proud. By month three, I was already standing a little taller because I'd been training my muscles to do it right. And so, I think that was received in a certain way with people. My body language improved.

Eventually, I reached the end of my trainer's expertise. And I recognized that familiar drive within me: I thirsted for more. Bryan had this broad range of experience compared to my shallow lane of physical fitness. He suggested, and offered to fund, a professional trainer in the bodybuilding world. He handed me a bio of a trainer he'd found and urged me to do a consultation with her. She'd been a bodybuilder for many, many years. And her efforts showed. She was stunning.

I knew immediately that I had to make an appointment with her — and I did — but I had anxiety for two solid days prior to our meeting. My head was spinning with fear around revealing this side of myself to her. Believe it or not, showing her my body was probably more uncomfortable than anything else I'd been exposed to in my life. She'd asked me to bring a bathing suit because we were going to be taking some before pictures.

I hadn't owned a bathing suit since I was a kid, so I panicked about that too. I wore a sports bra and a full-bottomed pair of underwear to our appointment, as it was all I had. I stood in a big posing room with the muscle-bound trainer in a super intimidating gym. As I listened to the determined clanging of the weights from the next room, I felt so mousy. I wore adult braces and had dyed my hair jet black. I acknowledged that although I'd worked out for a year; I was skinny-fat.

Looking at those first photos with that trainer today reveals that green undertone to my face because I was so mortified at being seen so up close and personal. I look frozen in fear: *Take the picture, take the picture, just take the picture!* It's ironic that I was uncomfortable to stand fit and sober before the trainer I was hiring to reshape my body, but I used to swing on a pole, half drunk, and crawl across the floor on a stage. Or hold a paddle, dressed as I pleased to cover any self-perceived flaws.

But when I was dancing or doing sessions as a FemDom, I was in a position of power. I decided how to approach a customer. I decided what to wear and when to wear it. I was not in a position of power at the gym: I was in a vulnerable space where others could see me. It felt too open to stand before that uber-fit trainer, and I nervously swallowed back my anxiety during the entirety of our first meeting.

When she explained she was going on vacation, we made a plan to work together first thing in the year. I asked for a meal plan, started it that next morning, and didn't go off for an entire twelve months: I was determined to reshape my physical body. I had already reshaped my mental and spiritual bodies, but no one could see the work I'd done. This time, my transformation would be visible to all.

I met with my trainer five days a week, even though I would feel physically nauseated in anticipation of leg day because it was so much work. Despite my prior year of light training, my legs weren't strong, so pushing the weight made me feel so light-headed that I would see stars. My trainer didn't go easy on me, and she wasn't supposed to. I paid her to transform me just as my clients had paid me to transform them; she did what she knew to do, just as I had.

When I learned that there was a bodybuilding show coming up, I mentioned it to my trainer and told her that I wanted to compete. She made one of those casual comments that have the power to wound the vulnerable, "Jewels, not everybody is made for the stage."

If we hadn't been standing in that noisy gym resounding with the clang of weights and feet hitting treadmills and grunts of effort, she would have heard the air leave my body. Her comment utterly deflated me. Our training relationship unraveled at that moment, and she soon lost a client because she voiced her careless opinion. I fought with that comment for a long time. I still recall it to this day, although it no longer has any power over me.

While working so intimately with a trainer, I developed an unhealthy relationship with her. First, she was in that intimate space with me, witness to my body, my mindset, my strength or lack thereof. I thought back to all the days I had been sensitive to men, despite my history with them. This showed me some people in the physical health world have not done adequate work on themselves. She should have known me better; and focused on calling out my strengths instead of her perception of my weaknesses.

Powerful people can still be my kryptonite. This woman had gained my trust too quickly; hers became The One opinion that mattered. I would have done anything she said, as I was so dialed into her that there was nobody else in the room. I trusted her a hundred percent and when our relationship fell apart; I mourned it as a divorce or a death.

Before long, I got locked in with another trainer and worked at a more extreme level. I had the addict approach: all or nothing. As I started coming into the body that I created, I went through many phases:

Get away from me.

This is my gym.

I will lift these weights.

I don't have time for you.

Go away; I don't want men hitting on me.

Don't tell me how to work out.

But as I grew into my body, I became more level-headed as I recognized the power I had. I don't mean the power to persuade, but I knew I had the power to love and be present in who I was. I loved to encourage others, because the reality is a few short years ago I took my first steps on the StairMaster. Knowing that I impacted others kept me motivated. I was mindful that our energy permeates, even when we're not aware of it. I was every bit as dedicated as I was before, but I learned how to balance things and not be extreme all the time.

Along the way, I became a certified personal trainer, and learned that just because I had a body didn't mean that I knew how to run it. All athletes have coaches, so it wasn't that I didn't know how to work or needed the accountability, but that I needed somebody to look in from the outside instead of the inside out when it came to where I needed to be critiqued. I needed the input. A second set of eyes.

Because I was part of a team, I embraced that team mentality. This coach trained in groups. So every morning at 10:00 the same 4–5 people would meet and he would take us through a weight-training regimen. It took away the idea that if I skipped a workout, nobody was going to know. Because I took pictures and sent them to my trainer every Sunday morning with a weigh-in, he would know.

And even more importantly, I would know.

In a few short years, I had completely dominated my own body and created it into something new. It's yet another transformation I'd undertaken in my life. The outside matched the inside. I could show two pictures — before and after — the green-faced Jewels in a workout bra and underwear and the Jewels proudly flexing in a string bikini. It feels good to have a comparison point — an external parallel to the choices I've been making internally for years.

I entered my first Physique Bodybuilding show at the age of 43, after training for two years. I was thrilled to take second place, and took home a medal. Even though there were only two of us in my class.

Oddly enough, after I competed in my first show, my ex-trainer came through the gym right afterward. She did not know that her casual comment had done so much damage to me, and I never told her why I stopped training with her. I told her I'd just competed at my first show. I'm not sure if it mattered to her, but it was a proud moment for me.

The second show I was 48. I got a new coach and trained hard but didn't do as great as I expected. But once again, I was thrilled to have accomplished such an amazing goal. I took 3rd place in my class. There were a total of nine of us. After the show, one of the judges reached out to my coach and suggested I do the last show of the year, but this time in the Figure division. The show was in exactly 12 days. I was elated by the idea of having a second chance.

I quickly made plans and met with a Figure posing coach in person and then remotely the Friday before I left for the show.

At the show, I was the first one to go on stage. I was so excited that I walked across with so much energy in me that I could have been doing hopscotch. Being on stage is nerve-racking. My heart pounded so heavily. I remembered only one set of the poses. And I did the wrong set. But I did that wrong set of poses with a hundred percent enthusiasm.

Weeks before my competitions, I shared my first trainer's

comment with my current coach and he too was astounded. When I got the affirmation that it was offensive to him too, I knew it was right for me to feel the way I did. Today I use her motto to get ready for shows: *Not everybody is made for the stage.* I say that to myself because at one time that remark had the power to cripple me. No more. And when I came off the stage with my first trophy in hand, my coach said to me, "Well, I guess she didn't realize you *were* made for the stage."

I beamed with pride. With my placing at that show I qualified for Nationals and I will compete for my IFBB Pro Card in September.

Although I competed in my first show at 43, it was just five years later, in 2020, that I competed in Physique Masters at the age of 48. Then it was suggested I move to Figure and compete again (12 days later) in a whole different division. I met with a Figure posing coach in person and then the Friday before I left for the show. This is where I qualified for Nationals for 2021. I guess I am the person who's made for the stage.

Bodybuilding was more than my time spent in the gym. My participation in AA helped me tremendously around my foray into the healthy lifestyle. For example, I learned that you are as good as the company you keep. A favorite saying of mine is that if you sit in the barber's chair long enough, you're going to get a haircut. So if I hung out with people who didn't eat well, I would start slipping. I would have a backlash, because I would slip further away from my highest self. I learned that this type of mental warfare that takes place is not a pleasant spot for me.

Anybody who starts to not eat well or puts on undesirable amounts of weight knows they shouldn't be doing it. They don't want to acknowledge how it directly affects their quality of life. Oddly enough, people have accused me of body shaming. If I prioritize reciprocal pleasure, I hate men. If I eat vegetables and lift weights, I hate myself.

One of my sponsors said, "One day you'll learn to love your body the way it is." I've also been told that because I was abused when I was younger, I must want to be physically powerful today so no one can harm me. I don't think that thought has even crossed my mind. I have always found it fascinating that people who aren't growing toward their highest potential feel responsible to psychoanalyze the people who are doing the work. If I wanted a therapist, I'd pay one; I've built a life upon the unproductive beliefs of others. It fuels me to be me.

People color their hair. They put tattoos on their body. They pierce their faces. They lay out in the sun. Bodybuilding is the way I celebrated and decorated my body. Nurturing my body is the way I enjoy being alive in the body that houses my soul. What I do with it is my responsibility, business, and pleasure. So, I define and take self-care very seriously.

I allow the negative comments to roll off my back. Yet any time someone admires my work, it gives me a sense of confidence. The older I get, I'm enjoying the idea that age is not working against me, but for me. At 49, I prepared for the Nationals bodybuilding competition. My sober brain has built a resilient, age-proof body and I gratefully praise the fact that I reached the age of 49, knowing that most people who experienced the things I did as a child would find it difficult to thrive. But I have overcome it all.

In public, people approached me and shared themselves vulnerably without wavering. They felt safe speaking with me. I prided myself on being authentic. I wasn't trying to be in somebody else's box. I built my body, according to me, and I was satisfied. Others saw that, and they felt inspired. I never mind taking a compliment now, because I am confident and I've earned it.

Before, when I was drinking and on drugs, I was not well-received. Admittedly, I was a complete nuisance. Too often I heard, "Do not come back here!"

Now, in the rooms of recovery, they say, "I'll see you tomorrow, Jewels!" My life is a story of transformation. I have all the humanness like everybody else, I have days that I don't want to eat my food. I have days that I'd rather have cake. I have the same internal committee, but on a spiritual level, I recognize my body as my temple. The way I could love myself physically was by sculpting it to something that best represented my soul. Strong. Brave. Jewels.

It's easy to drink and drug yourself down, but to build yourself back up takes so much more work. But Source was always there, the driving force behind everything; sustaining me throughout the miserable parts. And soon, after so much pain, I realized I had a choice. I could cling to motivation, self-care, and perseverance or I could stay broken, poor, and hopeless. So, I made the necessary, hard changes. I kicked the teeth of misery in and forbade it from ever taking up space inside me again. Every day, I woke up, and no matter how I felt, I made the executive decision to fight for myself.

Because I am Jewels — and I happen to my life.

CHAPTER TWENTY

-⁊|\‑

Outtalking the Tape

When my fifth summer with Bryan had arrived, we had a lot of separation and weren't playing as much anymore. Ms. Jewels' relationship with Juliette was changing. Though we shared a company together and I adored him, it felt like we were meeting our end. I had certainly reached a pinnacle, so the thought of change was challenging.

I went to my prayers. I had a conversation with Source where I said, "You have given me everything I've ever asked for. I live in a beautiful, high-end condo. I drive a Mercedes. My bills are not only paid, but I am no longer in debt. I have a slush fund. I have everything. But I have a big hole in my heart. You know me better than anybody. You know when I need things and I'm not questioning any of that, but I want somebody I could fall head over heels in love with. I'm completely at your whim. I'll do whatever that may be."

I had been faithful to Bryan for the duration of our relationship. Yet, on a Tuesday, I found myself behind the computer, making a dating profile. Within a couple of days, Matt reached out to me and answered all the fun questions I asked on the app. We agreed to meet in a nearby coffee shop.

Unbeknownst to Matt, as he waited for me in a coffee shop, Ms. Jewels was on her way to meet him. She walked in, wearing a suit and clicking her heels. Immediately, Matt's face went slack. He looked nervous, and he wiped a hand across his forehead more than a few times. So I did what I do best: I chose to shine even brighter.

I did all the things you're not supposed to do on a first date. I told the truth about who I was. I laid it out straight, as I had no intention of disguising myself. "First and foremost, I have a girl-friend. I will always have female romantic relationships because that is who I am. Also, I am the Vice President of a firm, and I have an erotic private life."

"Go on," Matt said, intrigued. He stayed. For the full date. And later said that he'd never met a woman with the caliber and the skills I had. Little did I know that as I was talking, Matt was learning, googling under the table on his phone to familiarize himself with all the terms I was throwing at him. The lifestyle. Head of household. Female dynamics. Female dominant. Open relationship. He was completely outside of his comfort zone. Yet he came into my life through the dynamics of Ms. Jewels. He was the first person I permitted to meet me exactly where I was at.

I said, "If you want to be a part of my life, you need to learn how to live it. There are two books that I highly recommend you read before we go out, *The Ethical Slut* and *Female Dominance*. These books will explain who I am and how I became who I am. They will explain life through the eyes of a female dominant."

Matt gave his word and before our next date, he had read both books — as if doing research for a job interview. This was a big deal to me, as I had to know I wouldn't waste my time with some-body who wouldn't accept me for who I was. I had learned in the rooms that there were places for me. I was insistent that my life moving forward was going to be one of them.

Next, I laid out the rules. "You must be prompt. If we go out, then you need to be at my door at exactly seven o'clock."

Then came the time when he was two minutes late at my door. When I opened the door, he was smiling, a bouquet of pricy flow-ers in his hands. "Good evening!"

"You're two minutes late."

"Well, here I am." As an executive, he was used to running a meeting or a business engagement with a confident smile.

"I told you I wanted you here," I pointed to the floor in front of my Christian Louboutin shoes. "Right here. In front of me. At seven o'clock."

"But I had to valet the car, and I had to check in with the concierge and it took them a little bit to get me up the elevator."

"None of those are my concerns. I said seven o'clock. I meant seven o'clock. Not two minutes after seven. Now there are going to be consequences."

He'd read the books, so he said, "Yes, I know." Perhaps he wondered what in the world I was going to do. But I let him off easy. That time. I wrinkled my brow at him as a smile slid across my face.

Matt looked visibly relieved. And he was never late again. He would drive over in his black Porsche 911 and park across the street from my high-rise. He'd either take a nap or catch up on emails, because he couldn't be late. He'd have a second shirt to change into and he'd brush his teeth to prepare for his arrival at exactly seven o'clock.

I asked Source for love, and when Matt presented himself, it was very clear that we would not have a strictly professional relationship. I could see right away that Matt had the qualities that I liked as a partner. And God said that I could fall head over heels in love with him as that's what I asked for. So when Matt presented himself, I just knew.

But then there was the time he propped me up on the counter of my fabulous high-rise and said, "I need to have 50/50 power if we're going to move forward in this relationship."

Sounds simple enough, right? Yet my heart dropped. I almost told him to get out, practically hearing my mom's voice about to scream from my mouth. I was torn because I finally found the power and the status of who I could stand in. And now this. I bit back all the words threatening to pour forth from my mouth.

That's not happening! You're asking me to relinquish my power to you? To relinquish my throne? Are you nuts? Do you not know who I am?

189

Were you listening? Did you not read the footnotes in the books? This is working for me. I can't be a homemaker. I've found my happy medium. And you're asking me to set that all aside and let you take the reins? Because that's what 50/50 means to me: the man leads the marriage.

I didn't give Matt an answer that night; I was too blown over by his request. I'd never considered an equal partnership and had no experience in that realm, so I couldn't agree outright. Truthfully, I didn't even know what 50/50 looked like; all I'd ever known was a man steamrolling over a woman.

But I'd asked Source for love, so I knew that what I was experiencing was supposed to be happening; I knew Source put people in our lives for good reasons. I asked Source for love, and he gave it, and now he was going to have to teach me how to have it. This required me to delve deep into what I believed about loving men. What did I have to bring to an equally yoked relationship? What did Matt have to bring? I knew he was something special, hand-delivered by Source. But my internal battles were fierce.

Then came the point where Matt said, "You know that you really don't have to work. I would rather have you travel with me and be by my side. This is what I need in a relationship right now."

Now this might sound like some women's version of a dream come true, but I panicked. I couldn't give up my clients and my high-rise in the sky. For what? To become dependent upon a man who could just up and leave when he wanted to? I had met Josh when his marriage was failing. I thought he was safe. He wasn't, and the downfall nearly took me out. No way could I play that game again. I was too mature to rely on another and too invested in my sobriety to bring instability into my life.

When Matt suggested that we try his suggestion for one year, we came to a compromise. I would travel with him for one year and then if I wanted to return to work, I could. Work was always going to be there. When it was time for Matt to do an around the world trip, he asked me to meet with him at the beginning. We flew to Hong Kong and then to Thailand. I was wondering, *What am I doing? I'm out on a limb again.* Then we arrived in Koh Samui,

where we were to stay at a super high-end resort Matt had arranged for us. As they drove us in a golf cart on a path winding
up to the top of the island to the resort that overlooked the sea of
Thailand, tears flooded my eyes.

As we checked in, the chef came running. "Mrs.! Mrs.!" he said,
and I thought, *Oh, let's not get ahead of ourselves here.* "I have your
meal plan. I can't get everything on the island, but I've done the
research to figure out what nutritional value I can replace the
unobtainable items with," he told me. He had this folder that
he'd been working on for weeks, chock full of notes. "My staff will
serve your food prep meal for your meal plan every three hours
as requested."

And it was true. No matter where I was or where I went, these
lovely people would make sure that I stayed on my meal plan. If
I was going on a safari or an excursion for four or six hours, they
would give me two readymade meals to take when I was leaving.

We spent a week bonding together, and it was fantastic. The
resort was so lovely and the energy amongst the Thai was the
same. I never wanted to leave. Matt knocked that trip out of the
park, proving to me that a relationship can balance on equal
footing. He could give: I could take. And vice versa, of course.

It wasn't a yellow brick to happiness, at first. There was turbulence as I removed my Ms. Jewels' mask. I was in a very vulnerable space where I hadn't had a lot of experience. I had the whole
front going on, including the Louis Vuitton bag, the downtown
castle in the sky, and I was driving the car. But — and this is a big
but — I had no experience with intimacy in my post-recovery
life. I was living on old tapes because they were the only thing I
had to fall back on. I could hear Mom in the back of my mind
saying, "Always have a Plan B, Jewels. Never relinquish all control to men. Always stand on your own. Don't rely on a man. As
Gloria Steinem said, a woman needs a man like a fish needs a
bicycle."

Trusting a man was fraught with risk. I had only my past to
peer back on, to realize that any trouble I'd experienced in life
had been at the hands of a man. Choosing to move forward with

Matt took more courage than perhaps anything I'd experienced up to that point.

Matt was separated when I met him. My moral compass told me that I would never infringe upon another partnership again. I would not date somebody within a relationship because I had done that every time before and it didn't work. Although I said that the agreement between others was no concern of mine, the potential for fallout was always there.

It was a big deal for me to go forward with Matt. I had to kill Mom's voice in my head. I had to give up power and control — and what was that word? — oh yes, I had to *surrender* to love. That's difficult for a woman like me to do. Yes, I could take a year to travel with Matt. But then, as we traveled to these fantastic places like Paris and London, no matter where I went, there I was. I was not a worldly person.

I didn't understand what was so great about Paris. In my infant mind of sobriety, I found Paris extremely overwhelming. There were people everywhere, rushing here and there, speaking in a language I didn't understand. Sometimes they were really loud. It triggered me to enact a barrier because when I couldn't understand what they were saying; I felt unsafe. I couldn't predict the room, let alone understand the verbiage like I would have been able to in my own culture. I experienced great levels of fear.

Matt suggested that I go shopping while I was staring at my pale face in the mirror, white-knuckling it at the hotel. *I'm not going out there. I'm not going out there by myself.* Back at home, my girlfriends were urging me to go party. To go shopping. To get on the train and take a ride to the next country!

Were they insane? Absolutely not. I couldn't even leave the hotel room without Matt. I'd look down from our window, down to the streets below. Not today. And I'd shut the curtains.

Well, what was I to do but to ask Matt for help? He was the only one in my scenario that understood what I was experiencing. I put on an almost therapeutic face, quelling the freight train of anxiety that was roaring through my head. I calmly whispered, "Uh, Matt, I have a tiny little bit of anxiety that I'm going to need some help with. I want to get out and do things, but I don't want to just roam around an unfamiliar city by myself."

Matt, ever the solution finder, offered, "Get on the city tour. All you have to do is sit at the top of the bus, put the earbuds in and allow the driver to show you the city." Perhaps this is what a 50/50 partnership looked like? I could express my vulnerability and Matt could rise to the occasion with a solution.

I first tried a city tour in London. I sat in a safe little spot on the top row of the bus and could see the beautiful parts of the area as I learned historical facts through the earbuds. And so I did that in different cities, moving forward, because that was the one thing I could do to bridge the gap to enjoy the gifts Source had given. Piecemeal, I moved forward to bring it all together. But it scared me to rely on Matt. Each generous offer meant to inspire security and safety in me instead created waves of anxiety and uncertainty.

At first, Matt wanted to move me into his family home and I nearly ripped the paint off the walls. "We are not living there! Are you nuts? Do you realize what the other women would do to a woman like me? There's going to be bloodletting at the cross. It's not happening." Matt is logistical, so I had to explain to him what life would be like for me in a neighborhood like that. I was not an executive wife. I was not a mother. I did not play tennis. I did not have a recognizable family surname.

Matt tried. He purchased a beautiful home for us, setting me up in the way he thought marriage was supposed to be set up. He bought me a nice home. I had my own bank account. He thought I was going to be thrilled, but he was wrong. I wasn't raising children, so that humongous suburban house felt like a jail. The extravagant house, meant to comfort me, instead elicited feelings of shame. It sounded great in theory, but I had no friends to share it with. I had no community. All the things that people usually did in a house like that weren't possible. I wasn't doing what normal people did with that kind of property.

193

Then, as we progressed in our relationship, some people in Matt's life discovered things about me that I didn't share with them. When they took it upon themselves to dig into my past and then share information with each other, Matt and I faced some uncomfortable confrontations. I've learned in life that when you hurt others, it will work against you. It may not be immediate, but it will happen.

There are different stages of rage. And perhaps Source was teaching me to learn compassion for others, while continuing to love myself and who I am. I could keep my cool despite the physical reactions as my body betrayed me. When confronted by family members, my body temperature rose. As I held my tongue, my lower jaw would visibly shake. Fire would shoot through my body as I swallowed my words and blinked back at what I faced before me. My body would do its own thing, but my poker face that could stay calm saved me every time. I didn't lash out or say anything unkind. God bless Mom, for raising me to be a better person than that.

I handled these confrontations with class, as I had learned to do. Some people aren't lucky enough to go through a recovery program that teaches them emotional regulation. I didn't lose my cool. I didn't give my power away. And it was miraculous to experience what everybody said I could actually do. When family members attacked me, I took the high road, and they stood down. I knew I could not spew my trauma onto Matt, because he was the man in the middle. I cared about his well-being. Any time I had something to fight about or get off my chest, I went to my girlfriends. His journey was addressing his relationships with family members. Those were not my relationships.

I had the wisdom from Ms. Jewels and working with men, I just didn't know how to interact with it on an intimate level. And over the course of our time together, I realized Matt and I were two wounded warriors doing our best to express ourselves, learning as we went. I'd absorbed various lessons through recovery and my work and in previous relationships. I understood a lot of things, but I needed to learn how to present it to a man who saw through different glasses than me. What couples normally process in a 15-year window, we did in five years. We catapulted, lesson to lesson, screaming through the air like two skydivers jumping from one life to another.

Sheer panic would send me flailing and we'd have to go back and work on it; then go back and work on it again. Each time Matt and I learned a new lesson together, Source would bring in a new level of healing for me and I would see the picture differently. That's how I have sexually evolved and became liberated in healing what was going on within me. Then I wouldn't feel old feelings or threats in my ideology of what it meant to be a man in these sorts of arenas. It's a process.

As for Matt, he had to learn to work with a feminine woman who could express herself. I don't manipulate around sex. I don't tell him to leave me alone and to go have sex with somebody else. This brave unknown world was new for him, too. Our relationship was solid, but it could be challenging at times because we're two very independent people.

The biggest lesson I have learned with Matt was stability in love, as he is so even-keeled. I could push. I could cat scratch. I could scream. I could say no. And he would never leave. There was a time when I was going through some uncomfortable revealing and he said to me, "Jewels, I will out-talk that tape."

When I woke up in the morning, he would look over at me and say, "I'm not going anywhere." The next morning, he would say the same thing. And the next. He constantly worked on the tape that I could not fight. I couldn't make it go away. God definitely gave me Matt, because I couldn't manipulate him.

When my heart — as opposed to my mind — felt comfortable, I stopped fighting Matt and the scary things he represented such as emotional security. Safety. Love. Bonding. Financial security. When I finally felt connected enough emotionally, I accepted that he was not going anywhere.

Although he gave me the house, the car, the bank account, it wasn't the financial element I was seeking. I could make my own money. I had to peel back more trauma and look deeper into myself. Why did I hold him at bay when all he wanted to do was love, support, and protect me? Isn't that what I always wanted? Wasn't the lack of those very things what had prompted me in the past to bring out the black garbage bags and hit the road?

My friends told me that they could see that Matt adored me. They asked me why I was fighting shadows that didn't exist and couldn't hurt me. They urged me to look at the big picture. And when I resisted, they pressed me to look again. It was that my insides were not matching what I was seeing on the outside.

When Matt stood up for me to a family member and said, "Jewels isn't going anywhere. If you will not respect her, then you won't see me either," it stopped me in my tracks. I have never had a man stand up for me. Not my fathers, not my boyfriends, nobody. Those words finally permeated my heart so I could believe that a relationship between me and a man was possible. That's what started changing my mind so my heart would accept it. It was never about the things. No, it was about the safety of being vulnerable and being accepted for exactly who I was.

When Matt asked, "What can I do when you're upset?" I told him that he just needed to tell me he loved me. Those words had the power to dissolve anger. It immediately diffused the emotional powder keg that was me. I don't know why. Maybe it was the energy that goes from my ears to my heart, but that's the one thing that will shut me down.

After undergoing surgery, I had a bit of a meltdown. During the recovery stage, I felt a little crazy. Matt walked in to find me sitting amid a pile of makeup and cream bottles on the bathroom floor. Matt's first words were, "How can I help?"

Oh, my God, you asked the question. Yes, I would love your help.

Since the beginning of our relationship, he has adored me and given me the gift of what it feels like to have a man remain present. He makes plans four months out in advance when I don't even know what I'm doing at six o'clock.

"Why do I need to know what I'm doing in September?" I'd ask him.

"Because I can't live my life on a whim. I have a career and a schedule to keep," he'd respond. I had to learn how to make plans, something I had little experience around. One time he said, "We're going to Cancun next week. We talked about it, remember?"

Matt has given me a space of safety. No matter what we go through, I can depend on him to roll over and say, "Jewels, I'm not going anywhere."

Nobody ever truly meant it, let alone say it. I've trusted before and learned that the love wasn't true. They left. Now I find post-it notes in my workout bag that I open at the gym.

You are amazing.

I love you.

You're my everything.

I'd do anything for you.

Matt is my happily ever after. My part two of life. It doesn't mean that I become stagnant and die. Or make babies and buy a house with a white picket fence. That's not my happily ever after, but this is.

CHAPTER TWENTY-ONE

Come Hell or High Water

For work, Matt only flew internationally, other than when he went to New York. The day he said he had a meeting in Chicago, I thought nothing of it, and he returned later that night, as he would for a business meeting. The week passed as usual, and when I called my dad on Sunday, as I did every weekend, he didn't sound like himself. I said to Matt, "My dad was kind of short on the phone today." Shrugging, Matt made an offhand comment that felt too nonchalant for my comfort. I had learned to trust my judgment by then, and couldn't understand why the two men I loved did not sound normal to me.

Several weeks later, I traveled with Matt to a spectacular resort in St. Lucia. The room had only three walls with the fourth wide open to the environment and the infinity pool. We'd been traveling all day, and I was famished. As I maintained a regular eating schedule because of my training, I needed to eat *yesterday*. We briefly explored the lovely room, and I mentioned that I couldn't wait another minute.

Then Matt caught me off guard. "First, I need to talk to you," he said.

"I can't wait to eat, Matt. You know that, can you just give me two minutes?"

He shook his head. "No, I have to say this right now. Sit down."

We'd already been sitting in a plane for hours, so I didn't understand why the conversation had to wait until my stomach was eating a hole in itself. So, I took a seat, half curious, half afraid. Anticipation wasn't something someone like me usually enjoyed.

Matt kneeled before me and said, "I have to talk to you about something."

"Okay." This didn't sound good.

He took a deep breath and said, "Remember when we said that we would always build our relationship on honesty?"

"Yes." My skin prickled. Panic started building in my body.

"Well, I haven't been honest."

Oh God. No. Please, no. Not another disappointment. "I'm listening."

"Remember when I said I was flying to Chicago?"

"Yes, I didn't realize you did business in Chicago."

"I don't. And I didn't really fly there. I lied to you," Matt said.

Here it comes. Wham. The 2×4 is going to hit me. Like always. Mom's voice sounded in my head. I told you, Jewels. Never trust a man. Never give up your power—

"I really flew out to visit your dad."

"My-my dad?" I stammered.

"I went to visit your dad to ask for permission." And Matt switched to one knee and opened up the jewelry box he brandished before me. "Will you marry me?"

I sat there, surprised, stunned, and most of all, silent. I was still stuck on *I wasn't honest.*

Matt looked at me. "Is . . . that a yes?"

"Yes, yes, of course, it's a yes! But wait a minute, you weren't honest?"

And then we laughed, and I made calls, only to learn that everybody knew about the proposal but me. Matt was not only a romantic, but an excellent planner and keeper of secrets. I called my dad and asked why he said nothing to me.

"Oh, Jewels, it was everything I could do not to tell you on our phone call. And that's why I had to cut it short. I can't keep secrets!"

Next, I called Melissa, my old sponsor. "Melissa, you're not

THE MAKING OF A WOMAN

gonna believe this!"

She asked, laughing, "Well, do you like it?" She told me that Matt had commissioned her husband to design the ring for me.

Oh, my God. Everybody knew!

✳✳✳✳✳

When I was much younger, I had allowed myself to dream. When I imagined my wedding day, it was always with my dad walking me down the aisle, as that was a gift that I wanted to give him as his daughter. Dad and his partner, Tonya, were not in great health and therefore could not travel, so we made the arrangements to have the wedding a month out on a boat near their home.

Matt and I flew back a couple of times to visit and make arrangements. During a visit to the florist, Tonya called and said, "Jewels, they've just airlifted your father to the hospital. He's having a heart attack."

I looked at the florist and calmly said, "I'm going to leave this in your hands. I need to take care of something." Matt and I drove an hour and a half out to the hospital. Dad was alive, but he needed to have a quadruple bypass. I stayed while Matt flew home to work and once again, as I had been with my mother, I was on hospital duty. Dad had another heart attack, and I prepared myself to lose him, thinking it was not fair that just like when he tried to take me from Mom and Robert at the fair all those years ago, we were one again *this close* to our happy ending.

When he recovered, Dad said, "Jewels, I'm gonna walk you down that aisle. Don't you worry." His voice was scratchy, weak.

"I know you are, Dad." It was the carrot I dangled, although our wedding was a few weeks away. Dad was stabilized and prescribed rehabilitation therapy once back at home, which was painful for him to do.

Tonya advised him to get to work on his rehab, or he was going to miss the wedding. "You have a daughter to give away, you know! You can't miss it." Her words spurred Dad to push through yet another painful challenge in his life. My upcoming wedding catapulted him through the pain of rehab. And one month later, he walked onto the boat, frail and weak. Nothing could have kept Dad from the honor of his role that day.

He walked slowly, but surely, wearing a scar and bandages under the slightly baggy suit he'd just purchased from Kohl's. While his body may have been frail, nothing could dim that look in my father's eyes. Dad looked happy and proud, the way he always did in my childhood memories. As we made our way down the aisle, he held onto my hand out of security and love. Tears ran from his eyes, as he said to me, "I told you, come hell or high water, I was going to walk you down this aisle."

Everybody in the room was in tears. You would have to be a statue to remain unmoved at the sight of that elderly man concentrating on each step forward. Chin held high, he marched me up to our friend who had become ordained to marry us. Dad was all smiles under his tears, anxiously pushing to give me away. Finally, there was a man — Matt — Dad felt comfortable giving me to.

And Dad, well, he finally got it right.

Matt and I said the vows we had each written, reflecting who we were. My vows were not about laws and rules. I proclaimed how grateful I was that Source brought an angel into my life. I vowed to do everything I could to protect our unity and our love. Matt's vows were traditional, but matched the beautiful way that Matt lives his life.

Even the sudden downpour of rain couldn't dampen the magic of our day. Matt and I worked together to get my dad safely off the boat, each of us supporting one of Dad's frail arms. Yet before we parted on that most magnificent day, we took a picture of my dad and me and later had it enlarged as a gift for his wall at home. Dad lived out the rest of his life with that photo he proudly displayed for all his visitors to see.

When I got sober, my mom died. And shortly after I married Matt, my dad passed on. I don't know if Source orchestrates our lives in this way, but as my guides completed their roles in my life, they were escorted to a better place. As I've said, we don't choose our family. But sometimes we sure get lucky in who Source puts in our path, even if their roles end sooner than we would have wished.

EPILOGUE

I understand, accept, and support that there are women who took a right when I took a left. It might be tough to explain my path to the other gals, though I do my best to understand theirs. They took the road they thought looked safe, which was to accept tradition, dogma, and their own tapes. They accepted the template: the dream of happily ever after.

Grow up.
Go to college.
Get married.
Have babies.
Retire.
Have grandchildren.

Recovery taught me to draft the template for my own dreams. We learned in the rooms that every situation is different; every person has their own pain to overcome, and hope to establish. We also must all figure out how to exist in a world that can be so challenging. My path wasn't easy. You could say I crawled across a lot of broken bottles to get where I am today.

While others walked the path that was expected of them, I struggled to get attached to somebody because I was afraid they were going to leave and that it would tear me apart if they did. That's my baggage. I came along with some pretty negative tapes. My mom left, my dad left. You didn't leave. But you abused me. Which means I wanted you to leave. It can be a mindfuck.

Relationships have trials, but we trudge bravely into areas

that some don't explore. I will not fight what feels natural to me. The things I do may be outside other people's norms, but I believe that Source made me exactly the way I am. If I hold that lovingly, and if it's not dirty to me, then I refuse to feel shame.

Looking back over my life, the shortest synopsis would be that tragedy struck and then I found Source. But the story is much longer, of course, and consists of many other details. Woven within my story is how I learned to work through my own limitations and ask for what I deserve. I learned how to integrate my true self into the world; to make a place for myself, when the world rejected me.

My goal in sharing my life is to help others distinguish the difference between man-made constructs and the Source that drives everything. Even if society grinds down the spirit, we honor ourselves by pursuing our highest good. That's on us to do.

The divine force that connects us all is unseen, yet Source can be powerfully experienced by the senses. By shutting down outside disturbances and going inward, you can connect. In meditation, you can listen. Allow yourself to be pulled into something greater instead of pushing myself to the limit.

Always be pulled. Never push.

It ends with us. Our no. Practice saying it because I promise it feels good. Instead of going for these easy expectations, I want to challenge you to sit in silence and lean into learning yourself. Only you have the power to change your life; only you have the answers to your questions. So grieve. Feel boldly and do not silence yourself.

Always be determined that the end of your story will be a powerful one.

After all, you are the author of your life.

ABOUT THE AUTHOR

I'm a woman who has lived two lives in one lifetime. The first part was a life of childhood abuse and trauma which grew into the full-blown disease of alcoholism. My life was out of control and I was circling the drain.

The second part is life today and how I urgently worked through my past and now have a wonderful life as a result. But my story is not your average *girl gets sober* story. I didn't just get sober. I created a life of truth and authenticity. My story is about removing the expectations and the dogma of society and instead being guided by love and empathy.

Some may call my life risky, unethical, and totally against the norm. But I see it otherwise. I'm in a very loving open-minded marriage, I'm sexually liberated because of my childhood trauma, and I'm about to compete in Nationals this year in the NPC Figure division at 49! Just a snapshot of my life today.

I've always enjoyed the work of Gabby Bernstein, Oprah, and Wayne Dyer. I would love to see my book as a supplemental reading in liberal arts classes, such as Women Studies, Sexual Relations, or Adolescent and Teen Psychology. But ultimately my target audience is the girl in the back of the room who feels she's the only one. She's the person I desire to reach.

I've had the honor of being a guest speaker on *Keys and Anklets*, a podcast focused on separating facts from fiction within often widely misunderstood lifestyles, *Pillow Talk*, another podcast that focuses on female-led relationships, and a documentary of alternate lifestyles broadcasted in the UK.

I would love to hear from you. Please reach out to me through my website, themakingofawoman.com, and my email address:
jewels@themakingofawoman.com